THE
IVY
LOOK

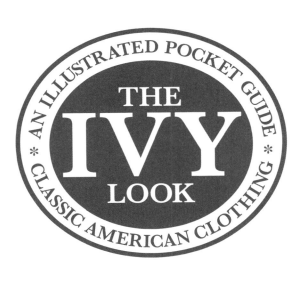

AN ILLUSTRATED POCKET GUIDE

THE IVY LOOK

CLASSIC AMERICAN CLOTHING

GRAHAM MARSH AND JP GAUL

FRANCES LINCOLN LIMITED
PUBLISHERS

For June, with love.   GM

For Astrid, Isabella and Joe.   JPG

First published in Great Britain 2010
Frances Lincoln Limited
4 Torriano Mews
Torriano Avenue
London NW5 2RZ
www.franceslincoln.com

Copyright © 2010, Graham Marsh and JP Gaul

A Natural Shoulder Production
Written by Graham Marsh and JP Gaul
Art Direction and Design: Graham Marsh
Page Layouts: Jack Cunningham

Graham Marsh and JP Gaul have asserted their right
to be identified as the authors of this work under the
Copyright Designs and Patents Act 1988.

British Library cataloguing-in-publication data
A catalogue record for this book is available from
The British Library.

ISBN 978-0-7112-3138-2

Printed in China
Cover Design: Graham Marsh

Opposite:
Miles Davis.
A detail from the
album *Milestones*.
Shown on page 68.

Following pages:
Steve McQueen
in the 1968
movie, *Bullitt*.
John F. Kennedy
in the early 1960s.

CONTENTS

FOREWORD

The Ivy look seems to us as fresh, exciting and relevant as ever and our aim in this book has been to reflect the history and the glamour of the style. Think of this book as Ivy League: 'The Director's Cut'. An entirely personal edit of what we consider to be the very best bits – the main styles, the sharp dressers and the major retailers.

It seems entirely appropriate that the authors came to learn and fall under the spell of the Ivy look through exposure to three quintessential American art forms – cinema, advertising and modern jazz. It is by exploring the most stimulating and compelling examples from these elements that the backbone of the book is formed.

Most of the images are from the prosperous mid 1950s and 1960s America, the decade when the Ivy look was at its height. We do this in a spirit of celebration and as a means for the contemporary reader to draw inspiration from an era rich in character and innovation. Like Dobie Gray says, 'The original's still the greatest!'

GRAHAM MARSH AND JP GAUL, MARCH 2010

Brooks Brothers, 1962.

THE IMPORTANCE OF BEING IMPORTED

Ivy clothes were addictive. I got hooked the first time I saw them being worn by the pilgrims of modern jazz who inhabited the London based art department of Marvel Comics where I first worked back in the early 1960s. It was an insider's world of narrow lapelled sharp Ivy suits, narrow knitted ties and narrow haircuts. The soundtrack to this cool, detached world was the music of Miles Davis, Gerry Mulligan and Jimmy Smith. This was a world I wanted into and like a sponge proceeded to soak up all it had to offer.

Apart from being a veritable running commentary of all that was happening in post-war graphic design, modern jazz album covers served another purpose. They provided a peerless photographic guide to the Ivy clothes that the musicians wore. Key parts of the Ivy mosaic were gradually dropping into place, the music was a given and as though seen through the lens of a Leica camera the clothes were coming into sharp focus. I was in a happy frame of mind.

Almost the only place selling Ivy clothes was Austin's legendary store at the Piccadilly end of Shaftesbury Avenue. Austin's sold exclusively imported American clothing from button-down and tab collared shirts to the Ivy-defining natural shouldered herringbone tweed jackets. All good stuff – but at a price. Later, the other serious contender selling traditional ready-made American clothes was called The Ivy Shop, the brainchild of John Simons, a modernist with a purist's take on the Ivy look. With his eye for detail, he succeeded in creating Ivy heaven by the banks of the River Thames in Richmond, Surrey. Times were good and Ivy wardrobes were full of the right stuff.

Needless to say, my first trip abroad was to America: not the European

Opposite: A template for the Ivy look. Paul Newman wears a corduroy jacket, khakis and sneakers in this 1956 off set photograph.

cities of Paris and Rome that were favoured destinations of my peers, but New York. Back then New York was Ivy Central, a modernist's Mecca, home of the button-down shirt and the Bass Weejun loafer, city of the sack suit and the legendary jazz clubs that made up the rich cultural life of Manhattan. Staying with American friends who had only just graduated from Rutgers University meant I had become, albeit temporarily, an Ivy insider. They introduced me to the campus way of life that included visits to Brooks Brothers and J. Press.

Brooks Brothers was something else; in the heart of New York, it was a vast, oak panelled emporium full to bursting point with the finest Ivy clothing, pared down and laid out on tables to be viewed as though works of art. To me they were just that, each label sewn in every garment that Brooks Brothers sold carried the words 'Made in USA', as reassuring to seekers of the Ivy look as an authenticated painting signed by Picasso.

The highlight of this trip, however, was an unplanned visit to the Village Vanguard on Seventh Avenue South at Greenwhich Avenue where the Bill Evans Trio were playing. Evans wore his standard-issue Ivy clothes with unconscious ease, his music understandably being of more importance to him than what he wore, but to me it was like an album cover come to life. It was 100% pure Ivy. The image was locked down and committed to the memory bank to be used for future reference.

In retrospect, like fine wine, I am glad I had the foresight to lay down a few of these early finds. Never to be replaced rare button-down shirts and Ivy jackets, worn to threads but now used as templates and duplicated by an understanding tailor. I can still enjoy wearing them in the knowledge they are one-of-a-kind. Nowadays it's harder to keep the Ivy habit fed but occasionally something surfaces that makes me smile and think – yes, that's it. And who knows, this book may inspire makers into again producing those much-coveted Ivy classics.

GRAHAM MARSH

Opposite: **No existentialist hit man would leave home without his trench coat. Alain Delon in the 1967 movie** *Le Samourai.*

LE SAMOURAÏ

PRODIS présente
ALAIN DELON

LE SAMOURAÏ

avec
FRANÇOIS PERIER
et
NATHALIE DELON

production
FILMEL - FILMS BORDERIE - T.C.P.
FIDA CINEMATOGRAFICA

Producteur délégué: EUGÈNE LEPICIER

Photo de: HENRI DECAE

un film de
JEAN-PIERRE MELVILLE

17 THE IMPORTANCE OF BEING IMPORTED

JOURNEY INTO IVY: A PILGRIM'S PROGRESS

The line goes that we are always curious about the world as it was just before we were born. In my case that's a 100% accurate statement. Born in 1964, the early 1960s have long captured my imagination, and as my later teenage years coincided with the myriad fashion crimes of the 1980s, I took delightful escape in some considered retrospective reappraisal. The world of the early Modernists was one that my friends and I studied and dissected with academic rigour. We bought the records, studied the pictures, mimicked the poses, but getting 'the look' right often proved difficult. It was the discovery of a pile of original late 1950s/early 1960s *Esquire* magazines in an antique shop which gave us the authentic building blocks upon which to learn about this mythical style we had heard people talking about – the Ivy League look! Another piece in the educational process took place when a series of original Blue Note records were reissued in those glorious pre-CD days: witness the cardboard sleeves! the heavy vinyl! John Coltrane's *Blue Train*, Lou Donaldson's *Blues Walk*, Freddie Hubbard's *Hub Tones*. That there was a harmony, such a strong connection between the music, the clothes and the sleeve design just seemed so clear. A style virgin, I was experiencing the alchemy of Ivy, that powerful cocktail of visual and sonic elements, for the first time. My hunger for more information and the need to be closer to the source led me on a pilgrimage to London.

It may only have been a small shop tucked away in what was, at that time, a

Opposite: 2 Russell Street, home of J.Simons from 1981 until 2010. This was the most recent manifestation of John Simons' many highly influential Ivy League clothing shops. The Ivy Shop, which was at 10 Hill Rise in Richmond, has become a part of 1960s folklore.

JOURNEY INTO IVY: A PILGRIM'S PROGRESS

rather quiet corner of Covent Garden, but John Simons' clothes shop became the fulcrum of a whole kind of scene. Here, held together by John's charisma and unique knowledge of clothes, men of all backgrounds came together to get hold of the very best of traditional American style Oxford cloth button-down popovers from Troy Guild, soft, finely tailored natural shoulder jackets from Linet, the G9 blouson jacket (christened the Harrington by John in the mid sixties), it really was all there. His selection and taste were peerless. The shop became a meeting place, part of a circuit that included places like Ray's Jazz Shop, Flip, American Classics, Valotti's Café and Dobells. At John's favourite films were discussed, style tips passed around, great jazz recommended and friends were made, including the two authors of this book. The shop's shoe cabinet rather appropriately resembled an altar and the item around which everyone congregated and gazed in awe at was the legendary Bass Weejun loafer which in the 1980s acquired cult status amongst many different types – inculding Soho trendies, Mods, rockabilly fans and graphic designers. And this I think is the true glory of the Ivy look, the reason I still wear it and cherish it. It is a wardrobe that bestows tradition and elegance upon those who were not born into backgrounds of tradition and elegance. It's a quiet, decidedly un-flashy way of communicating an appreciation for clothes with a connection to the great moments of twentieth century culture. It still means a lot to me that Miles Davis wore Bass Weejuns. I feel like I am part of that tradition. I am following in his footsteps.

JP GAUL

Opposite: Blue Train by John Coltrane, Blue Note Records, 1957. Photograph by Francis Wolff. Cover design by Reid Miles. An influential album for JP Gaul and many button-down types.

BLUE TRAIN

john coltrane

blue note 1577

SHOES
Stop talking, start walking: these shoes have soul

The first thing a member of the Ivy fraternity will look at are your shoes; from there they check out the rest of your wardrobe. If you are not wearing what are considered to be acceptable shoes you will be met with frosty indifference, at best a dismissive 'nice shoes' which you really do not want to hear. There are, of course, many types of classic footwear associated with the Ivy look.

For example, well-worn, low-tech sneakers such as Converse and Jack Purcell or a pair of Clarks desert boots will all guarantee automatic acceptance. However, when it comes down to the wire there are really only two tried and tested styles of shoe that have become the epitome of the Ivy look: the long wing-tip brogue and the loafer.

There is a scene in the 1967 movie *Point Blank* where Walker, the character played by Lee Marvin, is striding along the endless neon lit corridors of Los Angeles airport. He is there on a mission to take back $93,000 he was cheated out of by The Organisation. The camera cuts between his face and his feet. On his face is a menacingly impassive expression. On his feet are a serious pair of Florsheim Imperial long wing-tip brogues. They are five eyelet, Blucher-style with Goodyear welt construction in tan coloured scotch grain leather. Beautiful – you do not argue with a man wearing shoes like that. For the record, Walker gets his money and the film director Jim Jarmusch now owns Lee Marvin's size 13 Florsheims.

If *Point Blank* had the long wing-tip brogues the list of movies in which loafers were worn is endless. Gene Kelly sang and danced his way through

Opposite: Perhaps the ultimate American classic, the Bass Weejun witnessed a revival in the 1980s and was invariably combined with vintage big E 501 Levi's, Burlington argyle socks and a windbreaker jacket. Shades of James Dean. Very King's Road circa 1984.

An American in Paris wearing loafers, Fred Astaire had on loafers and a blue button-down in *Funny Face*. James Stewart wore loafers in *Rear Window*; Gregory Peck in *Roman Holiday* and Cary Grant raised the bar in *North by Northwest* wearing a pair of elegant tasselled loafers and a white button-down shirt, both courtesy of Brooks Brothers. Even Mathew Broderick wore loafers in *Ferris Bueller's Day Off*. Crazy. Loafers and button-downs – as American as apple pie.

The original loafer was introduced to America in 1936 by a bootmaker named George Bass, who had made boots for Admiral Byrd's Antarctic expedition and flying boots that Charles Lindburgh wore on his transatlantic solo flight. Bass, no novice when it came to footwear, adapted his new shoe from the traditional Norwegian fisherman's slipper, calling it the Weejun in acknowledgement of its Norse origins. Ironically, the Norwegian shoe itself was based on the American Indian moccasin.

The Weejun soon became a symbol of American casual style, worn by men and women alike. Women slipped pennies into the front and made loafers a fashionable craze. Indeed, Bass Weejuns are known as 'penny loafers' to this day.

That concludes a brief history of Bass Weejuns. Unfortunately for several years Weejuns have not been hand-sewn in Maine, New England, USA. They have the doubtful honour of now being made abroad, which does not seem quite right somehow. That said, designer Weejuns made in Maine have recently hit the stores. Sounds interesting but the authors think that if you own an original pair of Weejuns you should only wear them on high days and holidays, keep them in good order and if possible under glass.

There are still some long established outfits producing fine loafers in the USA such as Alden who make a superb, genuine, hand-sewn Cordovan moccasin. But when the powers that be instigate a museum of cult objects it will be a pair of vintage Bass Weejuns that take pride of place. These loafers have justifiably become part of Ivy folklore.

These are the shoes, Clarks desert boots aside, that need regular polishing, to be kept in shoetrees when not worn and, as and when the need arises, expertly repaired. A small price to pay for looking unapproachably correct, which is after all key to the Ivy Look.

85th Year

Bass
OUTDOOR FOOTWEAR

IN STOCK CATALOG

1961

G. H. BASS & COMPANY, WILTON, MAINE
Shoemakers Since 1876

G.H. Bass & Co., 1961.

'Wanna know if a guy's well dressed? Look down.'

George Frazier, The Boston Globe

G.H. Bass & Co., 1964.

A tribute to Roy Lichtenstein, who apart from his unassailable reputation as the godfather of Pop Art, was also a serious Ivy Leaguer. In his New York studio wearing khaki chinos, button-down and chambray work shirts he elevated the humble comic book frame to the level of high art. His paintings now sell for millions of dollars.

Above: G.H. Bass & Co., 1964.   *Opposite:* G.H. Bass & Co., 1965.

Bass

OUTDOOR FOOTWEAR
IN STOCK CATALOG

89th Year 1965

Bass OUTDOOR FOOTWEAR

G. H. BASS & CO., WILTON, MAINE
Shoemakers in Maine Since 1876

29 **SHOES**

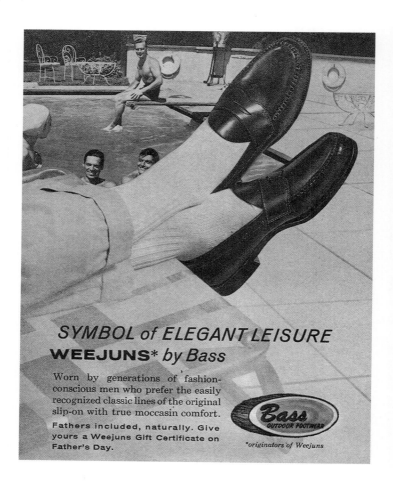

SYMBOL of ELEGANT LEISURE
WEEJUNS* by Bass

Worn by generations of fashion-
conscious men who prefer the easily
recognized classic lines of the original
slip-on with true moccasin comfort.

**Fathers included, naturally. Give
yours a Weejuns Gift Certificate on
Father's Day.**

Bass
OUTDOOR FOOTWEAR

*originators of Weejuns

G.H. Bass & Co., 1962.

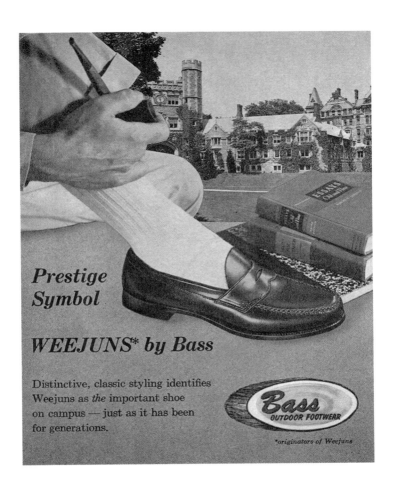

Prestige Symbol

WEEJUNS* by Bass

Distinctive, classic styling identifies Weejuns as *the* important shoe on campus — just as it has been for generations.

Bass
OUTDOOR FOOTWEAR

*originators of Weejuns

G.H. Bass & Co., 1962.

soft spoken lines

any man understands

.."With quiet authority, Bass Weejuns* go about your business from day to day, comfortable in the deepest sense of the word."

#450-in Tobacco Leaf Brown.
#451-in Black.
Both of subtle grain leather.

Bass OUTDOOR FOOTWERR

Originators of Weejuns*

G. H. BASS & CO., 41 Main St., Wilton, Maine   *T. M. Reg.

The story is not always so straightforward. Looking back we have a tendency to oversimplify the complex detail of the evolution of a style. Like the Florsheim Yuma with a chisel toe Bass here was no doubt responding to changes in the taste of its customers or perhaps the challenges posed by a competing shoemaker. The Weejun name has been stamped inside many variations on the loafer theme over the years. G.H. Bass & Co., 1959.

Suede loafers may not be to everyone's taste but suede loafers made by Cole-Haan are a very fine and acceptable addition to the Ivy look. Trafton Cole and Eddie Haan founded Cole-Haan in 1928.

An Ivy classic and favourite creation of Alden's brilliant shoemaker, Arthur Tarlow, the Alden Tassel Moccasin is a shoe of perfectly balanced proportions, comfortable fit, and simple elegance.

Guccio Gucci's most successful moccasin with the trademark snaffle vamp decoration on soft brown or black leather was introduced in 1953.They graced the feet of the elegant Fred Astaire and many other Ivy Leaguers. The Gucci loafer is strictly post collegiate and in summer should be worn without socks.

34 **THE IVY LOOK**

Entrepreneur Norman Granz put Stan Getz and Gerry Mulligan together for this 1957 Verve album *Getz meets Mulligan in Hi-Fi*. Apart from being formidable musicians Getz and Mulligan were fashion plates for a generation of Ivy Leaguers. Check out Getz's unbuttoned button-down shirt and the Sebago Beef-roll loafers that Gerry Mulligan is wearing in the photograph on the back of the album cover.

WINTHROP

MEN'S SHOES   *1962 Style Award Winner*

Squared off for holiday giving and holiday living,
THE MARK II, *from our Modern Living Wardrobe.*

Winthrop's exciting, new square-toe dress casual
that's so wonderful to give, to get and to wear during
the holiday season when the going's informal.
Fashioned over a square, chisel-toe last, with an elegant
hand-sewn front. In a wardrobe threesome of jet black,
coffee brown or coppertone smooth leather.

A product of International Shoe Company, St. Louis, Missouri

Opposite: Winthrop Shoe Company, 1962.   *Above:* Florsheim Shoes, 1960.

Florsheim long wing-tip brogues. From the Imperial range, the company's premium shoe. This cashmere Scotch grain brogue goes under the model name of Kenmoor. Milton Florsheim began producing shoes in a small factory in Chicago in 1892. The shoes Milton and his father Sigmund made were of the highest quality in style, comfort and workmanship. Florsheim were pioneers in developing national and eventually, international, distribution outlets through franchises and retail stores bringing shoes out of the back room and onto the sales floor on open display and in the fifties they sponsored celebrity golf tournaments. By 1966 there was a pair of Florsheim brogues sold every four seconds.

Opposite: 'I want my $93,000'. Lee Marvin as Walker in a scene from *Point Blank*, directed by John Boorman in 1967.

A selection of L.L. Bean's saddle shoes, another perennial Ivy staple.

L.L. Bean's rubber moccasin – still made in Maine from waterproof leather and rubber. The Ivy League shoe of choice for wet weather, often worn at outdoor gatherings in dry weather too.

The original deck shoe, the Sperry Top-Sider was an invention by a New Englander named Paul Sperry. The shoe gained legendary status when in 1939 at the onset of the Second World War the US War Department named the Sperry Top-Sider one of the official shoes of the Navy. In the 1960s, the Top-Sider finally came ashore and became essential footwear throughout college campuses – the ultimate Ivy seal of approval, which still holds firm today.

The Sperry canvas CVO. A classic since 1935.

Jack Purcell, the man behind the classic canvas shoe, was a world champion badminton player and one of Canada's leading tennis players during the 1930s. The sneaker he helped design became the athletic shoe of choice for on-court performance and casual wear. From coast to coast all across America the smiling logo on a pair of low tech Purcell's warms the hearts of Ivy Leaguers of all ages.

Chuck Taylor's All Star Converse high-top basketball boots and vintage 501 Levi's – they've taken over the world!

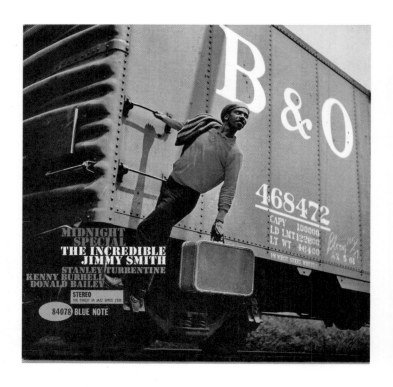

File under hip. Jimmy Smith's 1960 Blue Note album, *Midnight Special*. The photograph was by Francis Wolf and the cover designed by Reid Miles.

Unless you have an original vinyl copy of the 1960 Blue Note album shown opposite you may need a magnifying glass to see clearly the shoes that Jimmy Smith is wearing. It's worth the effort though as the master of the Hammond B3 organ has on a pair of plain front Florsheim Imperial cordovan loafers – this model was called Yuma. They had a hand-sewn front, genuine moccasin construction with leather sole and heel. These loafers were a 1960s Ivy classic and even better are still available.

Horween shell cordovan long wing-tip Blucher brogue.

New England's Finest. When Charles H. Alden founded the Alden Company back in 1884, shoe and boot making was a thriving industry in East New England towns. With the new invention of mechanised stitching and lasting operations, extraordinary improvements were possible in both quality and consistency. Before this the trade was based upon craftsmen making a pair of shoes a day in one-room cottages (called 'tenfooters').

Horween shell cordovan leisure hand sewn moccasin.

Number 1 Taunton Street, Middleborough, Massachusetts is now the home of The Alden Shoe Company, and still a family run business. In our opinion Alden's cordovan long wing-tip brogues and moccasins are the shoes that define the Ivy look. You can understand why in the 1960s trousers were worn slightly short of the shoe; no one wants to cover up a work of art.

SHIRTS
Button-downs, tab collars and the meaning of 16-34

The French novelist Gustave Flaubert once wrote 'Be regular and ordinary in your life, like a bourgeois, so that you may be violent and original in your work.' Miles Davis, the embodiment of hip and the coolest man on the planet during his Ivy suited period certainly subscribed in part to Flaubert's credo. On the cover of his 1958 album *Milestones* Davis subverted a standard issue garment that Joe College claimed his own by wearing an immaculate green oxford cloth button-down shirt. It was the Ivy look with attitude.

A host of new, young Hollywood Method actors such as Paul Newman, Steve McQueen, Montgomery Clift and the epitome of the Ivy look, Anthony Perkins, also favoured this comfortable, quintessentially American collared shirt. When starring in the Hitchcock movie *Psycho*, Perkins took care of business at The Bates Motel wearing a corduroy Ivy suit, desert boots and a white button-down shirt. He looked as sharp as his mother's knife.

The button-down shirt had come a long way from its origins on the polo fields of England, which is where, in 1900, John Brooks, president of Brooks Brothers, first saw that polo players had fastened their collars with buttons to keep them from snapping in their faces. Brooks took the idea back to New York where to this day it is the best use to which a sewing machine has ever been put.

George Frazier, the late, great taste master and columnist for *The Boston Globe* on the subject of the button-down shirt summed it up this way, 'The roll of the collar, that's the most important thing.' And, indeed, legend has it that only the long three and one-quarter inch points of the Brooks polo collar achieves the perfect roll. In

Opposite: An early 1960s publicity shot of actor Anthony Perkins. A clean-cut icon of the Ivy look Tony here sports the perfect button-down shirt in a miniature blue gingham.

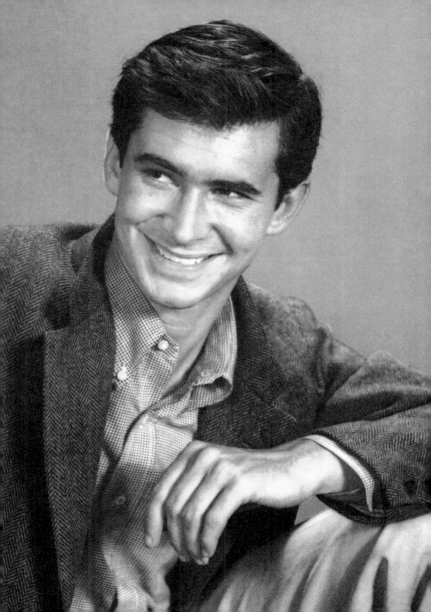

'The roll of
the collar, that's the most
important thing.'

George Frazier

one hundred and nine years four changes have been made to the Brooks Brothers button-down. Originally, it was a pullover shirt; this has been replaced by the coat style. A breast pocket was added due to the demise of the waistcoat. The back collar button is now history and in the late 1980s an extra button was added to the front placket which some in the Ivy fraternity considered unnecessary. One detail has remained constant: with a Brooks Brothers shirt, unlike many others, it is standard to find the correct sleeve length as well as collar size, 16-34 for example.

A close second to the venerated button-down is the tab collar shirt, which in the early 1960s was the shirt of preference for some Wall Street bankers and Greenwich Village sharpies. George C. Scott looked pretty mean wearing his tab collar shirt and narrow black suit playing a poolroom fixer in *The Hustler,* the movie that turned Paul Newman from a homeboy Ivy League actor into a star.

John F. Kennedy, 35th President of the USA, favoured the straight-point collared shirt worn with his trademark two button Brooks Brothers suit. This collar style also hits the mark when worn with a collar pin. The rounded or club collar has been an Ivy League staple since the 1920s although its popularity comes and goes. The English cut-away or Windsor collar and the English spread collar can sometimes be seen on Ivy Leaguers who have spent time in the UK. All of these shirt collar styles have merit but the Oxford button-down collar still remains the shirt of choice for pilgrims of the Ivy look.

THE BUTTON-DOWN COLLAR
The button-down collar is the essence of the Ivy look and is without doubt the most comfortable collar style. It perfectly complements the natural shoulder suit and tweed herringbone sports jacket. This shirt looks the business with a narrow knitted black silk tie or worn with the top button fastened without a tie. A look perfected by Bill Evans *(see page 73)*. The Brooks Brothers original all cotton Made in USA button-down remains the ultimate version. Accept no substitutes.

THE STRAIGHT POINT COLLAR
A basic staple of the Ivy wardrobe, known at Brooks Brothers as tennis point collar. The
favoured shirt of John F. Kennedy whose image makers lifted elements of actor Marcello
Mastroianni's cool Milanese style and grafted it on to the President's all-American look. Ideally,
the collar points should be between 2⅝ and 2⅞ inches long to balance the classic jacket
lapel. Add a pin to the collar and you have a passport to the Ivy look.

THE TAB COLLAR

This collar holds the tie in place with tabs attached to the collar and is fastened under the tie knot. These days the tab collar seems to be as rare as hen's teeth. This, however, was not always the case. In 1960s America, the tab, along with the button-down was considered the epitome of Ivy League style. If you still own an original tab collared shirt it may be worth insuring it against fire or theft!

THE ROUND (CLUB) COLLAR
Originally a mainstay of Eton School boys, this collar style has been a principal of the Ivy look since the 1920s although its popularity comes and goes. Can be worn with or without a collar pin.

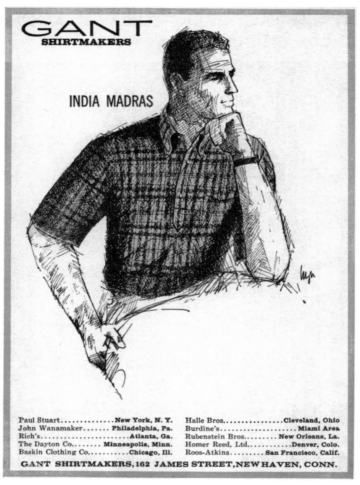

Gant Shirt Makers, 1961.

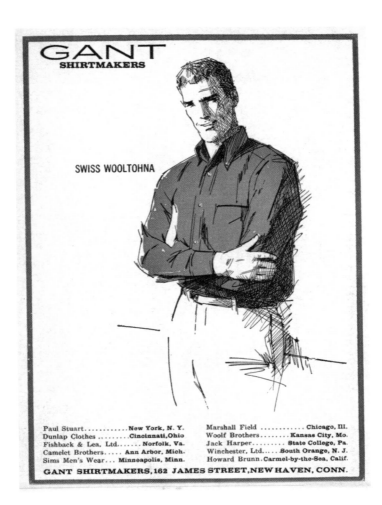

Gant Shirt Makers, 1959.

GANT

of New Haven

the Classic Favorite salutes "Ivy"

Take a collar with a gracefully flattering arched flare...add a button at the back and a comfortable back pleat...find a common denominator in proud fabrics from the finest American and foreign looms...and you have the Gant Button-Down. Wherever college men dress with distinction...wherever success-assured young executives foregather...there you will find this versatile favorite by New England's finest shirtmaker.

SEE THE GANT BUTTON-DOWN AT THESE FINE STORES:

New York......................Paul Stuart	Ithaca, N. Y...................Browning King	
Cambridge and Andover, Mass., Andover Shop	New Brunswick, N. J...................Luke's	
Hanover, N. H...................Dartmouth Co-op	Philadelphia, John Wanamaker University Shop	
Hartford......................Henry Miller, Ltd.	Providence......Harvey Ltd.	

or write Gant of New Haven, 162 James Street, New Haven for store nearest you

Gant Shirt Makers, 1959.

Gant Shirt Makers, 1964.

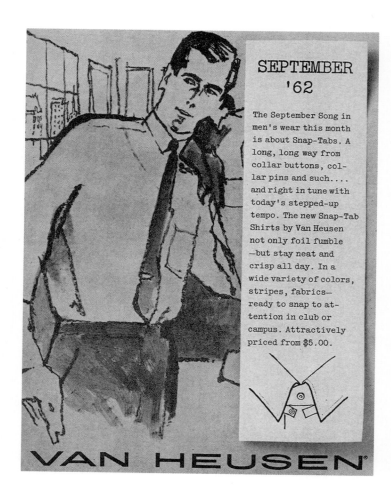

SEPTEMBER '62

The September Song in men's wear this month is about Snap-Tabs. A long, long way from collar buttons, collar pins and such.... and right in tune with today's stepped-up tempo. The new Snap-Tab Shirts by Van Heusen not only foil fumble —but stay neat and crisp all day. In a wide variety of colors, stripes, fabrics— ready to snap to attention in club or campus. Attractively priced from $5.00.

VAN HEUSEN

Van Heusen, 1962.

CURTIS AMY & FRANK BUTLER

GROOVIN' BLUE

CARMELL JONES · BOBBY HUTCHERSON · FRANK STRAZZERI · JIMMY BOND

PACIFIC JAZZ RECORDS

California dreaming. The button-down, collar style of choice for the discerning West Coast musician. Pacific Jazz Records, 1961, cover designed and photographed by Woody Woodward.

Above: h.i.s advertisement, early 1960s. A striking example of innovative and stylish 1960s American graphic design which also shows the incredible range of great Ivy clothing available in the period.

Opposite: Be as dapper as Dan and hip as Harry in one of these excellent madras shirts from J. Press, the world-renowned suppliers of traditional Ivy League style.

63 **SHIRTS**

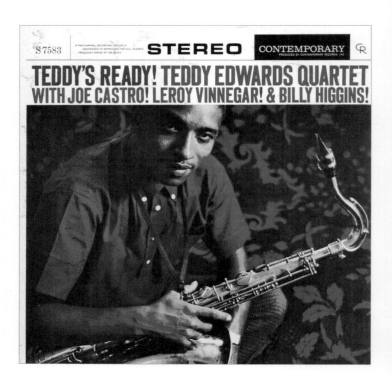

Teddy Edward wears a very fine button-down pullover, also known as a pop-over, shirt in this photograph by the legendary William Claxton for his album *Teddy's Ready!* designed by Guidi/Tri-Arts for Contemporary Records. The man in the Galey & Lord ad opposite also wears a very nice long-sleeve pop-over.

Jet Age View
of the newest in
sport shirts by

M*GREGOR®.

in "TOWN CRIER CHECKS"
Rich, masculine tones of
Burgundy and gray.
Styled for today
in Galey & Lord
two-ply cotton.

Galey & Lord Burlington

1407 BROADWAY, NEW YORK 18, N.Y.
A Division of Burlington Industries

Galey & Lord, 1960.

McGregor, 1964.

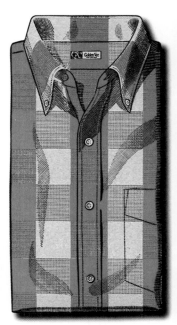

Golden Vee, 1964.

the
button down
TYPE

an informative but brief essay on shirts for campus and business

There is a far-flung fraternity of men whose badge is the button-down collar. Well-nigh fanatical on this subject, they shudder at the thought of being seen in any other kind of shirt. The ranks of this legion, not confined to Ivy halls, have infiltrated Madison Avenue, Wall Street and virtually all other strata of our society. For you who are campus bound, a goodly number of button-downs is of course a social must (how non-conformist can you get?). Truval has carefully assembled a collection of these collars all certified authentic. Represented here is the classic full-cut collar (left), as well as the shorter point version, most recent manifestation (center). They make their appearance not only in white, but in subtle colors and discreet stripes. And just to prove we are not narrow-minded, we have graciously included a new tab collar of considerable distinction (right). Like all Career Club shirts, they are taper-tailored with the new trim-waisted look. Somewhat stubbornly, Truval refuses to believe that good taste has to carry a high price tag. If you are more impressed by expensive labels than by solid value, that is your affair. But if you have a healthy respect for a buck, join the Career Club at your Truval dealer where fashion and value meet.

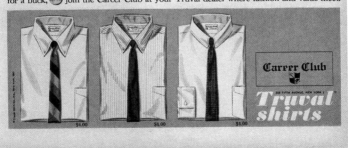

Career Club

358 FIFTH AVENUE, NEW YORK 1

Truval shirts

$4.00 $4.00 $4.00

Career Club, 1962.

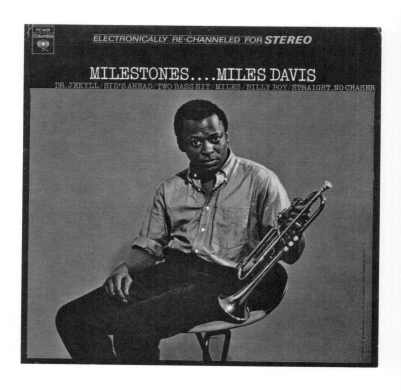

PC 9428
Columbia

ELECTRONICALLY RE-CHANNELED FOR **STEREO**

MILESTONES....MILES DAVIS
DR. JEKYLL / SID'S AHEAD / TWO BASS HIT / MILES / BILLY BOY / STRAIGHT, NO CHASER

Milestones — Miles Davis. Columbia Records, 1958. Miles Davis once asked a journalist who'd been watching him on stage how he'd done. 'You sounded superb' he replied. 'No, not that' Miles interrupted 'I mean, how did my suit look?' Image meant as much to Miles Davis as his very special music did. Miles became an icon of the Ivy look to such an extent that he was christened 'The Warlord of the Weejuns' by the great *Esquire* magazine style commentator George Frazier. If Miles wore it, it was instantly hip. Cover photograph by the outstanding Dennis Stock.

DEXTER GORDON bud powell/pierre michelot/kenny clarke

STEREO
84146 BLUE NOTE

OUR
MAN
IN
PARIS

Our man Dexter Gordon wears a rounded (club) collar shirt with a collar pin on this 1963 Blue Note album. Cover photograph by Blue Note boss, Francis Wolff. Cover designed by the peerless Reid Miles.

Richard Williams / Fred Jackson / Grant Green / Ben Dixon

STEREO

84174 BLUE NOTE

'The Way I Feel'

'BIG' JOHN PATTON

In the photograph by Francis Wolff, John Patton wears an iconic Ivy favourite, a candy stripe button-down polo collar shirt. Reid Miles designed the cover of this elegantly cool 1964 Blue Note album.

There is absolutely no use for the loop on this Creighton shirt!

Except in the locker room (athletes love it). So will you. All Creighton Shirts have plus details like the back collar button to keep your tie straight . . . and the box-pleated back for trim fit and comfort. The tailoring is decidedly natural shoulder with single needle sleeve construction . . . a further mark of quality found in all Creighton Shirts.

CREIGHTON SHIRTMAKERS
303 FIFTH AVENUE, NEW YORK 16, N.Y. MUrray Hill 3-5740

At Marshall Field, Chicago; Martins, Brooklyn; Stern's, New York City; or write us for the Creighton retailer nearest you.

Creighton Shirt Makers, 1962.

SUITS AND JACKETS
**Mr natural: narrow lapels to go,
hold the double-breasted**

Central to it all – the democratic, stylish and very comfortable Ivy suit, the origins of which can be traced back to those guardians of the Ivy League, Brooks Brothers, who else? In 1918 the brothers came up with their famous Number One sack suit characterised by unpadded, 'natural' shoulders, modest lapels with a buttonhole on the left, soft front construction, a centre back vent, and plain front straight-leg trousers. Basically, Brooks added a refined respectability to the baggy jacket and full trousers adopted by men in general earlier in the nineteenth century.

Although talking about jackets of a different kind, the photographer Francis Wolff, co-founder with Alfred Lion of Blue Note Records, once said of the label, 'We established a style, including recording, pressing and covers. The details made the difference.' It is the same deal when it comes to the finer points of the classic Ivy League suit – the details make the difference.

By the middle decades of the twentieth century many clothing companies such as Haspel, Chipp, and The Andover Shop were now making the ubiquitous, unstructured Ivy suit. These suits were the cat's whiskers, standard-issue production line numbers that even Savile Row could not match. It was during this period that those all-important details kicked in. The jackets were now half-lined and had raised seams. Another distinctive feature was the 6-inch, hooked back vent, although Brooks Brothers never had that legendary hooked vent on their jackets. The lapels

Opposite: The main man. Bill Evans was an extraordinarily talented pianist. With his trademark button-down shirt, top button permanently fastened, studious glasses and soft herringbone Ivy jacket, he looked like a Harvard professor of music. But do not be fooled – Evans was a solid musical innovator. Apart from playing piano on Miles Davis's unsurpassably influential modern jazz album, *Kind of Blue,* he also produced much sublime music as leader of his own various trios.

were narrow and for those members of the 'in' crowd who shunned conformity, only the top button of the jacket was fastened. The trousers of course, were plain fronted. Turn-ups or cuffs were the accepted one and three quarter inches (although some Ivy subscribers swore by one and five eighths, but that is another story!)

1955 saw the advent of clothier Joseph Haspel's synthetic, wash-and-wear seersucker suit that was claimed to be wrinkle-free. Many Ivy purists hated this look, complaining that man-made fabrics would never be as cool or comfortable as cotton. No surprise that dry cleaners sided with the purists. Brooks Brothers still make a polyester/cotton summer suit which if you want to chance it can be washed.

The east coast of America during the 1950s and 1960s was without doubt the spiritual home of the Ivy look. It was all about taking care of business, looking sharp within a pared-down, confident, modern America. From Barnett Newman's minimalist field of colour 'zip' paintings to Frank Lloyd Wright's beautiful Guggenheim museum and Eero Saarinen's design for the TWA terminal at Idlewild Airport, New York, the culture like the clothes exuded modernity.

For non-Americans, however, these cultural influences surfaced most prominently in the Ivy League clothing. It wasn't about the man in the grey flannel suit, more about those hipster saints that graced ultra cool modern jazz album covers – plus a few key television and movie actors. They were all wearing those highly coveted suits of dark blue hopsack, tan cotton poplin, blue striped seersucker and lightweight tweed jackets of brown and grey herringbone. The ultimate slice off the top had to be an olive drab, fine corduroy suit which when worn with a white Oxford button-down and black knitted tie could have you mistaken for either a visiting IBM executive or a sideman with a modern jazz outfit. Daydreams they may have been but these clothes were a righteous celebration of the Ivy look. They were imported and correct to the last patch and flap pocketed detail. As one head-to-toe Ivy wearing friend of the authors maintains, there is no substitute for digging the clothes you wear.

Opposite: **A still from the film** *The Graduate,* **1967. The college boy look here has such a timeless feel. This is a textbook corduroy Ivy jacket combined with dark green polo shirt and blue jeans that have faded to the optimum shade. Little wonder the Robinson girls found him so irresistible.**

THE CLASSIC CUT FOR JACKETS

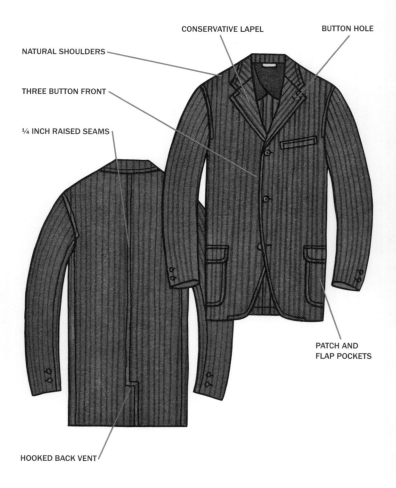

CONSERVATIVE LAPEL

BUTTON HOLE

NATURAL SHOULDERS

THREE BUTTON FRONT

¼ INCH RAISED SEAMS

PATCH AND FLAP POCKETS

HOOKED BACK VENT

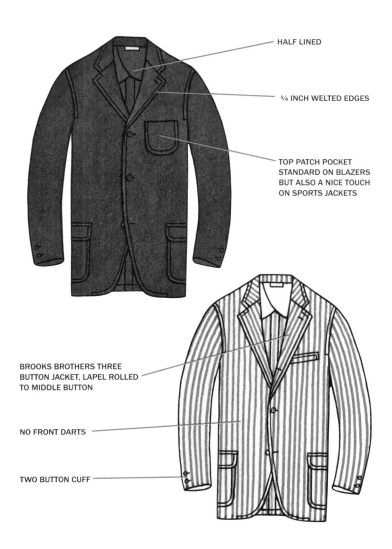

HALF LINED

¼ INCH WELTED EDGES

TOP PATCH POCKET
STANDARD ON BLAZERS
BUT ALSO A NICE TOUCH
ON SPORTS JACKETS

BROOKS BROTHERS THREE
BUTTON JACKET, LAPEL ROLLED
TO MIDDLE BUTTON

NO FRONT DARTS

TWO BUTTON CUFF

Cricketeer, 1964.

be the man
you want
to be!

Get revved up
and go in the
new 3-piece

CORDUROY CONVERTIBLE

You're every inch a man in this
easy-going sport outfit that's actually
"a wardrobe-in-itself!"
Natural-shouldered jacket lined
in an Antique print has
a jaunty matching breast-pocket
handkerchief. You'll go for the
center vent, hacking pockets and Antique
crested metal buttons, Post-Grad
slacks are pencil-slim, plainly terrific.
Rounded vest reverses to match jacket lining
and handkerchief. Wear the Convertible
everywhere — in all kinds of
combinations — you'll never look
better in your life!

The 3-piece Convertible . . . $29.95
Reversible vest alone . . . $5.95
Post-Grad slacks alone . . . $6.95

For a colorful 17" x 22"
Sports Car poster to pep up
your bedroom, dorm or den —
send 25¢ to H·I·S, Dept. ES,
230 Fifth Ave., N. Y. 1 —
to cover cost of postage
and handling. For set of
6 posters (6 different
sports) send $1.50.

ACTIVE MEMBER
SPORTS-CAR
CLUB
SPONSORED BY h·i·s

h·i·s
SPORTSWEAR
Don't envy H·I·S . . . wear them

h.i.s. sportswear, 1960.

The Basic College Wardrobe. *Esquire,* September 1962. 'Jackets have natural shoulder (no padding), three button closure, center vent and straight hanging lines. Shirts: 6 white button-down oxford cloth, 3 blue, 1 yellow or olive and 3 striped; 2 tab collars in white.'

'Shoes: 1 pair black or brown moccasin slip-ons, 1 plain-toe cordovan, 1 black wing-tip laced shoes, 1 rubber-soled gym or tennis shoes. In general these are the clothes that a well-dressed college man would have.'

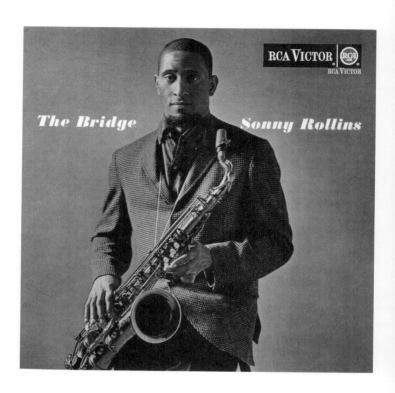

Above: The saxophone colossus returns. After a three-year sabbatical getting his musical chops together Sonny Rollins makes his comeback in style. Shaved head, goatee beard, sharp jacket and great shirt. Mr Rollins has it all on this 1962 RAC Victor album photographed by Charles Stewart.

Opposite: Anthony Perkins looking sharp in this studio portrait by Bud Fraker taken around the time of the 1960 Hitchcock movie, *Psycho*.

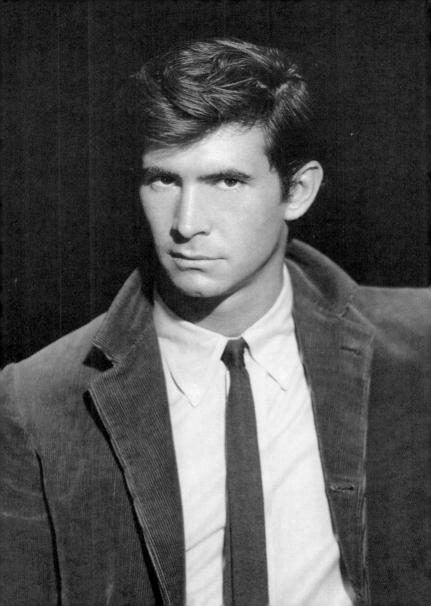

LUCKY YOU ... IN THE WORLD'S LIGHTEST SUIT!

Yes, you, in the amazing 6 oz. Dacron-worsted suit by Clipper Craft. Lightest, coolest summer suit ever! And one of the smartest, thanks to a rich measure of New England tailoring. The heat stays out, the press stays in, you stay immaculate. At the 1318 men's stores, coast to coast, that pool their purchasing power in the Clipper Craft plan to bring you outstanding value. And what an impressive variety of patterns!

STEP OUT OF THE SWELTERING CROWD, INTO MR. COOL! $45.95

CLIPPER CRAFT

MR. COOL TAILORED EXCLUSIVELY BY CLIPPER CRAFT, 18 STATION STREET • BOSTON 20, MASS.

Mr Cool meets Mr Cool. *Opposite:* Paul Newman. *Above:* Clipper Craft, 1959.

ATLANTIC 1254

the
jimmy
giuffre
3

Above: William Claxton took the cover shot of the always elegantly turned out Jimmy Giuffre Trio for their 1956 Atlantic album. See the trio in the 1958 movie by Bert Stern, *Jazz on a Summer's Day* and know the meaning of cool.

Opposite: Raeford Worsted Company, 1962.

Behind every great suit is a great fabric!

RAEFORD'S FINEST WORSTEDS BECOME GREAT SUITS BY VARSITY-TOWN.

Only the most outstanding fabrics meet the standards of Varsity-Town suits—"Pacemaker for Smart America." So Varsity-Town chooses Raeford's "First Honors" worsteds. No finer fabrics have ever been woven in America, or anywhere else. Trust the manufacturer whose suits are made of Raeford worsteds. He uses great fabrics...to give you great suits. Raeford Worsted Company. A division of Burlington Industries, Inc.

Raeford

© 1964 Burlington Industries, Inc.

With characteristic originality,

Gordon of Philadelphia

varies a theme with

tattersall check trousers and

solid coat in new Field Olive tones.

Of Galey & Lord

Dacron* and cotton.

Galey & Lord

1407 BROADWAY, NEW YORK 18, N.Y.
A MEMBER OF BURLINGTON INDUSTRIES

*DUPONT'S POLYESTER FIBRE

Galey & Lord is a textile mill founded in New York City as a partnership by Charles E. Lord and William T. Galey in 1886. They sought out new fibres, finishes and processes to create entirely new types of innovative fabrics. They are still the largest producers of premium twill and corduroy in the US. Galey & Lord, 1959.

Galey & Lord, 1962.

From Gordon-Ford...

the imperturbable

Dacron* polyester and cotton suit

in miniature British checks,

for resort and right through the summer.

Galey & Lord
1407 BROADWAY, NEW YORK 18, N.Y.
A Division of Burlington Industries

*DUPONT T.M.

Galey & Lord, 1961.

Summer in seersucker—Eagle Clothes plans cool comfort in a boldly striped Dacron* polyester and cotton jacket.

Galey & Lord

1407 BROADWAY, NEW YORK 18, N. Y.

A Division of Burlington Industries

*DU PONT T.M.

Galey & Lord, 1963.

Old Grads

Seersucker graduates, with honors. *Esquire,* May 1962. 'A favorite of the Club and Campus set. The old grads prefer the classic grey-and-white stripes in Dacron-cotton. Traditionally cut jackets have natural shoulders, three buttons, pleatless trousers. Deansgate, about $45, Paul Stuart, NY. To the right, in a class by itself, the new look of seersucker.'

'Left to right: an Arnel-and-cotton seersucker blazer, ribbon-striped. Natural shoulder styling. Roman-striped in a dozen sun-drenched shades, an all-cotton seersucker sport shirt with button-down collar. By Sero. About $8'.

Above: There is a definite collegiate feel to the location and the Ivy clothes that Bill Evans is wearing on this 1966 Verve album cover photographed by Chuck Stewart.

Opposite: Musical genius Quincy Jones wearing the perfect seersucker jacket circa 1962.

95 **SUITS AND JACKETS**

ORIGINAL VINTAGE CLOTHING LABELS

As good as a piece of contemporary Ivy clothing can be, there is often nothing that can quite touch what an original item from the fifties and sixties offers. The charm of an old Ivy jacket or shirt is often enhanced by the delightful vintage clothing labels sewn inside. Many were ornate and rather beautiful, witness the h.i.s design above, many included the name of the town of the manufacturer, and they all carried the 'Union Makers' stamp which proudly alerted the consumer to the fact that these goods had been assembled by proper organised American labour. Good old eBay and a few other specialist websites still make these items available. They're normally very affordable and are always unerringly evocative of a bygone and rather special time.

Clipper Craft, 1957.

Deansgate, 1962.

THIS SHORT INTERVIEW WITH RALPH LAUREN WAS FIRST PUBLISHED IN *NEW YORK* MAGAZINE – OCTOBER 1985

Q: I guess you're more than partially responsible for the preppy rage...

A: Brooks Brothers was the foundation, and I revived it. I worked for them and wore all their clothes; I also left them as a consumer when they started making Dacron and polyester. They no longer had a style, and I was a traditional guy. So I saw the opening in the whole market and said, 'Well, I want to look like this, and I don't want to shop here anymore. They're not moving.' They did change, but they became more ordinary, more mundane. I was not going to be high fashion, but I did believe in individual sophistication, a more customized look – what Brooks Brothers used to be when they were great. That was what I went after, what I love, which is a life-style. Men who had a lot of money would go into Brooks Brothers to buy shirts, and say, 'Give me three white, three blue, and three pink,' and they'd walk out. They'd do it every year, year in and out. They weren't interested in what was the latest this or the latest that. I recognized a certain mentality and security about them. Working there was like going to an Ivy League school; there was an 'in-ness,' a quiet 'in-ness' about that kind of place.

Opposite: Although made in 1977, Diane Keaton and Woody Allen effortlessly personify the East Coast Ivy look wearing clothes by Ralph Lauren in *Annie Hall*. Woody Allen was no novice when it came to the Ivy look; he'd been wearing those clothes his entire career.

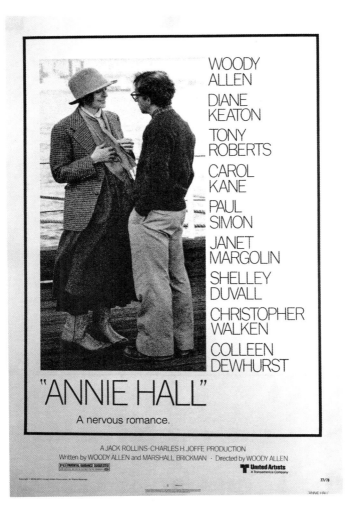

TROUSERS

Ivy trousers are *always* flat front no matter what the fashion pundits tell you

Most Ivy Leaguers nowadays insist upon natural fabrics for their clothing, which obviously includes trousers. Not a thread of Polyester or Velour infiltrates the Ivy wardrobe. However, this was not always the case.

In the early 1950s to the mid 1960s the only game in town was a pair of high-waisted, Sta-Press trousers made from one of the new synthetic 'miracle' fabrics such as Dacron, which was developed by DuPont. This material was lightweight, wrinkle resistant and easily laundered. These trousers were plain front, always worn slightly short of the all-important shoe and had narrow straight legs with a one and three-quarter inch cuff, or turn-up. The belt loops were narrow and did not drop below the waistband. Most had pockets that opened along the side seam, although in the 1960s when some brands of trousers became tighter and narrower belt loops were dispensed with altogether and cross or frog pockets made access easier. Those Dacron days may be long gone but there is no doubt about it, wearing Sta-Press trousers while relaxing in a 1956 Charles Eames black leather and rosewood lounger is a good look.

Even though the basic shape of Ivy trousers has not changed much since those halcyon days there is really only one style that has transcended the decades to become a veritable passport to the Ivy look – the khaki drill cotton chino. You can wear them loose and baggy, frayed and worn, with or without a crease, paired with sneakers or loafers. They look good with an oxford cloth button-down tucked in or shirt tails flapping in the breeze, walking along a beach on Martha's Vineyard or Brighton, depending upon your travel budget. Khaki chinos were and still are eminently versatile. Best, if you can track them down, are a pair of 1950s standard-issue US Army button fly all cotton

SLACKS SHOWN: 55% "DACRON"™ POLYESTER FIBER, 45% WORSTED WOOL. *DU PONT'S TRADEMARK. DU PONT MAKES FIBERS, NOT FABRICS OR CLOTHES.

"DACRON" LETS YOU RELAX IN SLACKS...WITHOUT WRINKLING

Did you know "Dacron"* was a fall-weather friend, too? Take these slacks of "Dacron" polyester fiber and worsted wool. (You can for just $17.95.) Comfortable. Good-looking. Dependable, too. Because they let you relax, have fun, yet stay well-pressed, well-dressed. And in any weather. Snow. Sleet. Slush. More: these ideal fall-weight slacks have a stain-repellent finish for extra neatness. Colors? You'll find all the favorites. Where do you find these fall-weight slacks? See opposite page for the store nearest you. Handsomely styled and tailored by *Seven Seas*

SEAFAST

BETTER THINGS FOR BETTER LIVING . . . THROUGH CHEMISTRY

Seven Seas, 1962.

khakis – they do not come much better. Like the man said 'They're so square they're hip.' One very important detail to remember – front pleats never appear on Ivy trousers. They are *always* flat front no matter what the fashion pundits tell you.

Other important Ivy fabrics for trousers are wide-wale corduroys and grey flannels, best worn with a navy blazer. White cotton canvas trousers worn with a madras jacket look pretty sharp. Seersucker cotton trousers are good on their own but much better as part of a summer suit. Oxford cloth, another summer weight fabric, usually comes lined. If you must wear wool plaid pants make sure they are in authentic tartans only. And of course, Nantucket Reds, a brick red cotton canvas when new, will fade to a beautiful cherry pink in time. They look good worn with most shirts and great with a Lacoste. Sperry Top-Siders or L.L. Bean moccasins on your feet finish this essential East Coast look – just remember to ditch the socks in summer!

THE CLASSIC CUT FOR TROUSERS

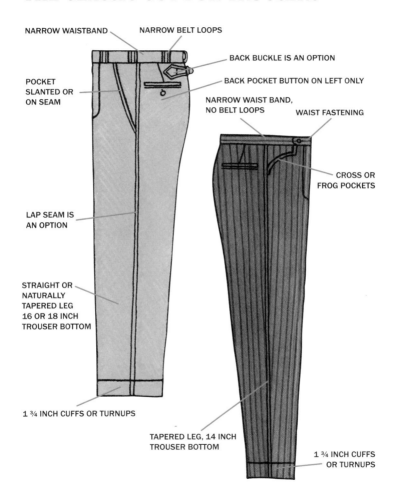

NARROW WAISTBAND

NARROW BELT LOOPS

BACK BUCKLE IS AN OPTION

POCKET SLANTED OR ON SEAM

BACK POCKET BUTTON ON LEFT ONLY

NARROW WAIST BAND, NO BELT LOOPS

WAIST FASTENING

CROSS OR FROG POCKETS

LAP SEAM IS AN OPTION

STRAIGHT OR NATURALLY TAPERED LEG 16 OR 18 INCH TROUSER BOTTOM

1 ¾ INCH CUFFS OR TURNUPS

TAPERED LEG, 14 INCH TROUSER BOTTOM

1 ¾ INCH CUFFS OR TURNUPS

The Preppy elegance of the Kennedy brothers defined the Ivy look; even off-duty they got it right. In this 1967 photograph by Steve Schapiro, Robert Kennedy plays touch football wearing a pair of well-loved khakis, sneakers and a US Navy issue G-1 leather flight jacket.

SLIM SLACKS SHOWN WITH ESQUIRE'S "BRIGHT LIGHT" COLORS FEATURED FOR '55

The slim line in slacks takes over

Biggest single trend of '55 in men's clothing is the natural slim line
from head to heel. This clean, straight cut completely replaces
the rippling roominess of yesteryear's sportswear—puts your full-cut
slacks among the family antiques. The time is ripe. Put on this
lean, attractive look in dress slacks and inexpensive washable pants.
You'll find that the good buy in *any* price bracket is equipped
with the equally streamlined Talon trouser zipper.

Talon

THE QUALITY ZIPPER

TALON, INC., MEADVILLE, PA. • IN MEXICO, CIERRE DELAMPAGO S. A. DEC V. • IN CANADA, LIGHTNING FASTENER COMPANY, LIMITED

Talon, 1955.

This is ~ HERITAGE

Traditionally styled from fine woolens, supple leathers with English Brass or English Pewter buckles!

$4

Hickok, 1962.

h.i.s. Sportswear, 1961.

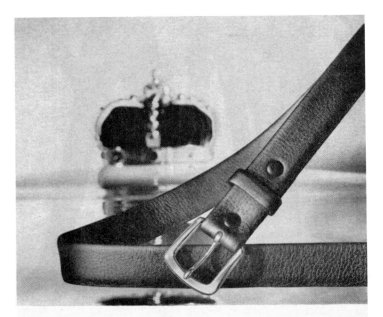

Glove leather

PRIDE · MARK

belt masterpieces by Paris

First, Paris® selects a breed of cowhide inherently supple and pliant, and by an exclusive tanning process, gives it a soft richness that typifies the mellowness of glove leather. Ask for style 505, just $5.

Paris Belts, 1957.

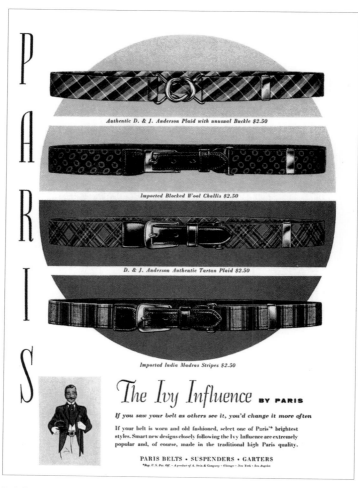

Authentic D. & J. Anderson Plaid with unusual Buckle $2.50

Imported Blocked Wool Challis $2.50

D. & J. Anderson Authentic Tartan Plaid $2.50

Imported India Madras Stripes $2.50

The Ivy Influence BY PARIS

If you saw your belt as others see it, you'd change it more often

If your belt is worn and old fashioned, select one of Paris'* brightest styles. Smart new designs closely following the Ivy Influence are extremely popular and, of course, made in the traditional high Paris quality.

PARIS BELTS · SUSPENDERS · GARTERS
Reg. U. S. Pat. Off. · A product of A. Stein & Company · Chicago · New York · Los Angeles

Paris Belts, 1957.

keep
that
fresh-
out-of-
the-box
look
with

Vycron®
POLYESTER FIBER

Vycron is the registered trademark for Beaunit's polyester fiber.

Seven Seas puts a smile in summer fun—and comfort—with these Summertide slacks. Tailored to make you look lean and trim, the slacks are sure to keep their just-bought look. That's because the fabric, by J. P. Stevens, is a wrinkle-shedding blend of 55% Vycron polyester/45% Narco® high-tenacity rayon. Slacks are completely wash 'n' wearable, need little or no ironing. Fabric performance is certified by Nationwide Consumer Testing Institute. In 15 sunshine colors. Sizes 28-44, about $11. Also available in walk shorts, about $9. At fine stores listed on page opposite. Or write Moyer Company, Youngstown, Ohio. ● **Beaunit Fibers**, Division of Beaunit Corporation, 261 Fifth Avenue, New York 16, N. Y.

Seven Seas, 1963.

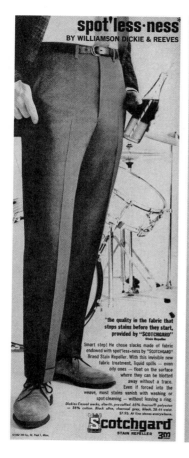

spot'less·ness*
BY WILLIAMSON DICKIE & REEVES

"the quality in the fabric that
stops stains before they start,
provided by "SCOTCHGARD"
Stain Repeller

Smart step! He chose slacks made of fabric
endowed with spot'less-ness by "SCOTCHGARD"
Brand Stain Repeller. With this invisible new
fabric treatment, liquid spills — even
oily ones — float on the surface
where they can be blotted
away without a trace.
Even if forced into the
weave, most stains vanish with washing or
spot-cleaning — without leaving a ring.
Dickies Casual slacks, slim-fit, pre-cuffed, 65% Dacron® polyester
— 35% cotton. Black olive, charcoal grey, black. 28-44 waist.
$7.95. At fine stores everywhere.

Scotchgard
STAIN REPELLER **3M**

DO $5.95 SLACKS GO WITH A $45 SWEATER?
(You'll agree they do when the slacks are Tapered Lee-Lustre Twills)

Don't let the trim tailoring, the rich subtle
textures fool you. Lee Tapered Slacks
really do cost less than six dollars. Yet,
they're perfectly at home with the
most elegant sweater or sports jacket.

Above, classic tapered Lee-Lustre
Twill slacks with cuffs and belt loops in
Sand Beige. Sanforized Plus for Wash
and Wear-ability. Also in Lee-Lustre
Sateen fabric. Priced at only $5.95.

Leesures by Lee

Dickies, 1962.

Leesures by Lee, 1962.

There are 3 completely new ideas in this picture!

LEVI'S SPORTSWEAR . . . a new slack concept. Both Continental and Ivy league styles have that smooth, smart look that makes these slacks favorites for all activities. They'll look as good at the end of the day as they did when you put them on. That's because the rugged "Royal Grizzly" fabric with Avril rayon takes hard wear in stride without muss or fuss. *Guaranteed for one year.* Levi's Sportswear is so convinced that you'll really like these slacks that they are making this guarantee. In black, loden, brown and beige. Men's sizes, $7.98. Boys' sizes, $5.98 and $6.98. At stores near you, or write Levi Strauss, 1 West 34th St., N.Y.

AVRIL...the most advanced rayon known to man! It's the strongest rayon ever made for men's wear. And this Dacron® polyester and Avril® rayon blend shows this amazing new fiber off to the very best advantage. For Avril makes possible the remarkable feeling of luxury . . . the unflinching way this fine-line gabardine takes to hard wear . . . gives it the very best wash and wear qualities, too!

A new class of American automobile. Only in "Avanti" by Studebaker will you find this modern school of design. It's like an aero-dynamic wedge designed to defy the wind. Luxuriously fitted-out, it is the fastest American production car now on the road.

AVRIL . . . a revolutionary new AVISCO® RAYON

AMERICAN VISCOSE CORPORATION, 350 Fifth Avenue, New York 1, N.Y.

Levi's Sportswear, 1962.

A pair of original 1950s US Army-issue khakis. Like Dobie Gray says, 'The original's still the greatest!'

Less is more. The renowned American fashion illustrator Betty Brader managed to capture the shape and feel of the bongo player's chinos perfectly on this 1956 Fantasy album by the influential vibe player Cal Tjader.

The outstanding artwork David Stone Martin produced for book and record covers defined 1950s American illustration. He was the best. Much copied but never bettered. This evocative 1955 Verve album cover is a classic.

Camel, 1963.

Haggar Slacks'
free expansion waistband
caters to the active man—
in Galey & Lord
2 ply Dacron* polyester
and cotton.

Galey & Lord

Burlington

1407 BROADWAY, NEW YORK 18, N.Y.
A Division of Burlington Industries   *DUPONT T. M.

Galey & Lord, 1962.

MODS
London calling: the original Ivy suited Modernists make the scene

The year was 1960. It was like powering up the grid after a blackout. Suddenly the monochromatic austerity that had enveloped London since the end of the Second World War was once again connected to the light source and into this cool spotlight stepped the Modernists.

These original Mods came of age in a time of full employment; they were young, financially secure and all day long thought of nothing but Bass Weejun loafers and American Ivy jackets. We are not talking here about those later Carnaby Street 'Swinging London' Mods but the knowing young working class kids and an army of art students all with finely tuned cultural antennae aimed overseas at America and Europe. They had looked over London's fence and liked what they saw; there was no going back. Those formative influences were for life.

You had to be cool. You had to look cool. The way you stood, the way you smoked a cigarette and the music you listened to were all-important to the clothes-obsessed Mods who inhabited the London of the early 1960s.

Haircuts from France, scooters from Italy, clothes from America, all nailed down with a laconic London attitude. The importance of being imported applied to the clothes as much as to the music. While modern jazz and the soul that poured out of the Stax, Atlantic and Motown record labels was required listening, the desired look for those discerning Modernists was strictly Ivy League.

Before John Simons, who by his own admission was no Mod but an Ivy

Opposite: No room for squares. Georgie Fame was the Modernists' musician of choice. He sounded like Mose Allison, played the Hammond B3 like Jimmy Smith and worked Blue Beat and Motown into the mix. He played to capacity crowds at London's Flamingo Club and with his Madras jacket, tab shirt and Bass Weejuns he had the Ivy look nailed down to perfection.

League clothing obsessive, opened The Ivy Shop in the autumn of 1964 at 10 Hill Rise, Richmond, the outfits selling genuine Ivy clothing were severely limited. Tracking down those narrow lapelled herringbone Ivy jackets and striped Career Club and Gant button-down shirts pre The Ivy Shop meant a trip to Austin's, situated on London's Shaftesbury Avenue, which because of its Americophile showbiz and media clients was very expensive.

After The Ivy Shop followed a succession of three other London shops selling traditional American clothing: The Squire Shop in Brewer Street, The Village Gate in Old Compton Street and J. Simons in Covent Garden. However, John Simons will be forever known as the man who sold and promoted the incomparable Baracuta G9 jacket. He coined it the 'Harrington' after the character Rodney Harrington, played by Ryan O'Neal, who wore the G9 in the 1960s TV soap opera, *Peyton Place*. The jacket needless to say was the star. The Harrington became a Mod staple along with all the other button-downs, tabs, long wing-tip brogues and loafers that Simons sold.

By the mid 1960s, after the boneheaded violence kicked off on the beaches of Brighton and newspapers grew tired of incorporating the word 'Mod' into any and every front page story, they gradually became history. This suited the original Ivy clad Modernists who like many previous instigators of influential cultural movements had moved on taking their sensibilities and clothes with them. They melted into the background like well-dressed CIA sleepers surfacing every now and then to throw a few sartorial comments in the direction of those who get it badly wrong.

The boot that kick-started a thousand scooters. Sixty years ago Nathan Clark gave to the world the timeless Clarks desert boot. He modelled it on a type of boot made in the bazaars of Cairo and worn by off-duty British Army officers. In the 1960s from American College campuses to the streets of London's Soho, it was the *only* boot to be seen in. With its uppers of smooth full-grain suede and plantation crepe soles it's a fine looking example of the shoemaker's art.

THE CLEAN WHITE SOCK

They think you're wacky but they always think you're right. That's because you're "clean white sock"; the convincing way you have of doing what you please. Adler socks are your favorite because they go along with you on anything. Here all feet wear the Adler SC shrink controlled wool sock. $1.00.

ADLER THE ADLER COMPANY, CINCINNATI 14, OHIO   IN CANADA: WINDSOR HOSIERY MILLS, MONTREAL

Adler Company, 1962.

Get in with the 'In' crowd! Scooters were the Italian way of getting from A to B in achingly cool style. For both Ivy wearing London Mods and American hipsters – distinguished only by their accents, the scooter was *de rigueur*. The Shetland crew-neck, pipe-smoking, white socked man favours the Lambretta while our flat cap and be-suited 'Jazz Beaux' digs a Vespa.
Album cover by Norman Gollin.

Who used the arrow motif first; Blue Note Records or the Mods? Who knows, who cares? It works, that's all that matters. Francis Wolff's photograph and Reid Miles' design make this Blue Note album from 1964 a stone cold design classic.

You can guarantee that on any Mod compilation CD there will be at least one track from Mambo master Cal Tjader. Mister Tjader wears a very tasty herringbone Ivy jacket on the cover of this Fantasy album from the late 1950s.

THIS IS OUR MUSIC

THE ORNETTE COLEMAN QUARTET

WITH DONALD CHERRY / ED BLACKWELL / CHARLIE HADEN

ATLANTIC 1353 FULL *dynamic frequency* SPECTRUM

The Ornette Coleman Quartet were pioneers of what came to be known as Free Jazz.
Although their music was not to everyone's taste, legions of Modernists bought the record
just for the cover, simply because the quartet look so damn sharp. This excellent 1960
Atlantic album was photographed by Lee Friedlander and designed by Push Pin Studio
alumni, Loring Eutemey.

THE CANNONBALL ADDERLEY QUINTET AT THE LIGHTHOUSE

RECORDED "LIVE" AT THE LIGHTHOUSE, HERMOSA BEACH, CALIFORNIA

FEATURING NAT ADDERLEY

344 RIVERSIDE

Another solid Mod favourite was the Cannonball Adderley Quintet. Imported albums and American magazines such as *Esquire* and *Downbeat* provided an invaluable visual guide to the correct clothes to track down, or get copied by a tailor who understood the importance of the small details that made the difference. The very laid back Californian photographer William Claxton took the picture used on the cover of this 1960s Riverside album designed by Ken Deardoff.

AN IVY LOOK FOR ALL SEASONS
Spring forward, Fall back

Ironic really, given that shoes, shirts and jackets are probably the three defining elements of the Ivy look, that in this section we find so many key components of the style. Starting with sporty summer wear the polo shirt has long been part of the aspirational WASP wardrobe, going right back to Rene Lacoste's invention in 1926 of the short sleeved pique cotton shirt with the soft flat collar and two button placket (an early example of Continental Drift – the US-Europe wardrobe dialogue). Get seven of these in navy blue and remove the stress of decision making during those lazy summer days and nights. And to really capture that beachside look don a pair of flat-fronted shorts falling just above the knee in khaki or madras. At the coast this look is topped off perfectly with a pair of Sperry Top-Siders but you can urbanize it by swapping Sperrys for Weejuns. Totally acceptable at the beach in Cape Cod or sipping espresso in Bar Italia. The exposed ankle has to be the ultimate visual metaphor for those Ivy League notions of moneyed leisure and relaxed elegance. Once the sun starts to emerge discard the socks.

The choice of knitwear is similarly straightforward and uncomplicated.

Opposite: East Coasting. President John F. Kennedy aboard the US Coast Guard yacht *Manitou* off the coast of Maine.

We know what works and we sure as hell know what doesn't. Has a man ever worn a simple crewneck Shetland as well as John Fitzgerald Kennedy does in the picture on the previous page? The perfect, athletic fit, the great neckline, the studied nonchalance. He is wearing the sweater – period. Crew neck, Shetland, mid-grey. Other colours can look good – Shetlands are tough to find these days but do often come in delightful heathery shades. The V-neck and high-buttoned cardigan (not too baggy now or you cross dangerous waters) are the other styles that work. And we shouldn't forget the classic knitted three button polo practiced today so perfectly by John Smedley of Derbyshire. Long-sleeved in merino wool or a nice twist in short sleeves and Sea Island cotton in summer. Just a few more words on that Kennedy picture and one in particular that is overused but here is so apt – *sprezzatura*. He sports the perfect casual Ivy wardrobe. The Persol sunglasses, the Yves Klein blue polo shirt, the khakis, the sneakers. Perhaps above all it's the fit that brings it all together – hats off to Jack! 10 out of 10.

Coats. It gets a bit trickier here. There is disharmony in the Ivy ranks. Men of a certain vintage go weak-kneed at the very mention of the original 100% cotton Burberry trench coat, the Trench 21. They point to the great Jean-Pierre Melville films like *Bob Le Flambeur*, *Le Samourai* and *Le Doulos* as proof of the greatness of the coat. Some hark back further to the great film noir period in which the trench coat and American cinematic style became intrinsically connected. And it is undeniable that these are great coats, beautifully made and loaded with authenticity.

But there is another school of thought that finds the more functional single-breasted raincoat preferable. Still made by Burberry or Aquascutum, and churned out back in the day by the likes of London Fog and Alligator, the slimmer aesthetics seem to harmonise well with the simple shapes of the rest of the wardrobe. There is consensus over other outerwear possibilities, amongst which the finest are the pea coat, made today by many good American manufacturers, including Sterling Wear and Schott, and the duffle coat, still made to exacting standards by Gloverall, the British manufacturer. Get them as heavy, basic and original as you can and you'll have an indestructible set of timeless Ivy threads.

Love him with
Puritan Ban-Lon® Brookviews
of DuPont Nylon

Give him America's favorite knit shirts. Full-Fashioned.
Automatic wash and dry. In 25 amorous colors. $8.95 each.

PURITAN®
THE PURITAN SPORTSWEAR CORP., 135 W. 50TH ST., NYC

Where to buy it? See last page.

Puritan Sportswear, 1962.

THE CATALINA® MAN *discovers* **Creslan**®
ACRYLIC FIBER

For the golfer who takes his sports and sportshirts seriously, this handsome
lightweight shirt is knit to fit in 70% Creslan acrylic fiber, 30% nylon. It lets
a man swing with comfort. It dries into perfect shape after laundering.
In sporting colors, about $12.95. Cyanamid makes the Creslan acrylic
fiber; Catalina makes the garments. American Cyanamid Company, New York.

Catalina, 1960.

Inside the advertisement:

SHEFTON— chukker shawl collar pullover—$16.95

MARIO—convertible shawl collar pullover—$15.95

MONACO— heavy-rib boat neck pullover— $15.50

ELMORA—basket weave pullover with club collar— $16.95

CHALFIELD— cardigan coat sweater with metal buttons— $18.95

SEE THE BULKY

You'll go for these Puritan beauties in a big way! They're 100% pure wool! These natural wool wonders have an especially nice-to-be-next-to texture, a talent for keeping their shape for all of their long and handsome life. See them yourself in season's smartest colors (nothing takes color and clings to it quite like wool). Get into a Bulky wool Puritan today.

NATURAL WOOL KNITTED IN AMERICA

Puritan Sportswear, 1960.

Time to get the long <u>and</u> short of summer style

Talon, 1956.

Van Heusen, 1962.

Classic walk shorts from J. Press, the company that along with Brooks Brothers epitomises the Ivy look. J. Press continues to offer its clients an up-to-date version of the classic American style it helped to create.

Puritan Sportswear, 1964.

True Blue. Pass muster at any off-duty Ivy gathering in a pair of 501 XX Levi's and a Lacoste. No point in making life complicated. This pair is 1955 vintage.

The all cotton Lacoste tennis shirt with its cap sleeves, narrow collar and two button placket
front is the Ivy sports shirt of choice.

A John Smedley label adds that prestige hallmark of quality to the Ivy wardrobe. The Derbyshire knitwear firm, founded in 1784 by John Smedley and Peter Nightingale, great-uncle of Florence Nightingale, has become synonymous with fine quality and timeless design. *Above:* John Smedley short sleeved summer classic fine knit polo shirt in Sea Island cotton. *Opposite:* Jerks Socks, 1962.

SUBJECT: SMARTNESS IN SOCKS! GRADE: EXCELLENT!

It's a foregone conclusion. You'll make the collegiate scene in a big way wearing this quality BAN-LON® sock. Narrow ribs for a new look of slim neatness. Cushion sole for comfort. The co-eds will flip over the thirteen campus-approved colors. 100% "Textralized" nylon in one fit-all size. **$1.50.** Jerks Socks, Inc., Cincinnati 6, Ohio

Jerks Socks
The Sock of Socks

CAMPUS AUTHENTICS' *College Board has approved Manhattan Shirts, Wembley Ties, Jerks Socks and Keystone Cameras.*

Above: On this 1958 Riverside album cover photographed by Paul Weller and designed by Paul Bacon, hipster saint Chet Baker wears a very eclectic mix of Ivy clothes including an unusual funnel neck sweater. *Opposite:* Pendleton, 1962.

AUTHENTIC PENDLETON®

An American Classic

. . . and tickets right on the Fifty. Both are solid campus favorites. For nearly a hundred years now the Pendleton people have made the vitality of 100% virgin wool their stock in trade. Here, a bright new, neatly casual pullover with button-down collar. The jacket is for the man who takes his leisure in comfortable stride. Authentic Pendleton . . . dyed, spun and woven in the Northwest—by people who make quality a tradition. Pullover Button-down Shirt, 14.95; Slacks, 23.95; Topsman Jacket, 22.95.

ALWAYS VIRGIN WOOL

For additional information, write Dept. E-12, Pendleton Woolen Mills, Portland 1, Oregon © 1962 PWM

Willis & Geiger's
perennial—
anti-freeze
Northland Parka
in a
winter-resistant
cotton
by Galey & Lord.

Galey & Lord

1407 BROADWAY, NEW YORK 18, N.Y.

A Division of Burlington Industries

Galey & Lord, 1962.

Zero King's challenge to the great outdoors: a sturdy, full-length stormcoat with detachable pile lining. Of subdued plaid in a weather-repellent Dacron* polyester and cotton fabric.

Galey & Lord

Burlington

1407 BROADWAY, NEW YORK 18, N. Y.
A DIVISION OF BURLINGTON INDUSTRIES

Galey & Lord, 1962.

Your
Alligator
goes
with you
everywhere

Alligator Stormwind®—most outstanding value in finely woven cotton poplin. $19.95. Also with zip-in all wool plaid and zip-in luxurious pile warmers slightly higher.

You'll always look your best in an Alligator coat! Available in smart styles and colors in fabrics of the finest all wool worsted gabardines, finest colorful wools, finest yarn dyed multicolor cottons in gabardines, poplins and woven patterns—also blends of natural and polyester fibers—all water repellent—and waterproofs, too.

See America's most wanted coats, from $11.95 to $70.75 at better stores everywhere.

Alligator
THE BEST NAME IN ALL-WEATHER COATS AND CAR COATS
The Alligator Company • St. Louis, New York, Chicago, Los Angeles

Your
Alligator
goes
with you
everywhere

SANSTORM® Smart new styling—extra fine cotton gabardine. $22.95.

For every man, for every occasion, for every kind of weather. Good-looking smart styles, excellent fit—all wool worsted gabardines, fancy wools, finest yarn dyed cottons in plains and woven patterns. Also blends with Eastman Kodel polyester, DuPont Dacron polyester, Courtaulds Topel cross-linked rayon. All water repellent. Fine Dacron waterproofs, too. America's most wanted coats. At better stores everywhere—$11.95 to $70.75. **Alligator**
THE BEST NAME IN ALL-WEATHER COATS AND CAR COATS

The Alligator Company • St. Louis, New York, Chicago, Los Angeles

Alligator, 1962.

Alligator, 1962.

News from
Scotland—
International
Tweed Coat...
magnificent orlon fleece lining. New leather
trim, "Weather-Leash" closure $59.95.
New Norther lambswool and Shetland sweater
$10.00. Silk 'n' cotton sportshirt $10.00.
Forstmann Benara luxury-wool flannel
slack $25.00.

From Sweden—Polar Seagull
Coat; Princeton striped nylon
fleece reverses to Travis-woven
nylon taffeta. Jumbo-knit
collar and cuffs, wash 'n'
wear $25.00. Shirt—Match
Top Tartan buttondown $5.95.
Slack—Ivy Haven Flannel,
no pleats $15.00.

WIDE, WIDE WORLD

McGregor searched every corner of the globe—no matter how
remote—for new, interesting fabrics—handsome,
dashing designs. The Continent, the Tyrol, the East, the Arctic,
Scandinavia...all represented on these pages.

Yes, the accent is definitely international...
and with McGregor as translator, a whole new world of
global-inspired fashion awaits your inspection!

McGREGOR

SPORTSWEAR Made in U.S.A. Also boy-sized, boy-priced. **McGregor-Doniger Inc.,** 303 5th Ave.,N.Y. 16, N.Y. *T.M.

McGregor Sportswear, 1960s.

Pianist Horace Silver taking it easy in his classic Burberry 'Trench 21' trench coat. 1956
Blue Note album cover photographed by Francis Wolff and designed by Reid Miles.

the
ornette coleman
trio
at the
"golden circle"
stockholm
volume one

BLUE NOTE

It's cold in Sweden but Ornette Coleman braves the snow in a very fine, slightly shorter length trench coat for this photograph by Francis Wolff. Reid Miles designed the 1965 Blue Note sleeve. The layout of the type was quintessentially American and was used by Reid Miles to great effect on many Blue Note album covers.

There are two theories as to the origins of the US Navy pea coat. Firstly, that it originated from the Dutch *Pijjekker* – *Pij* being a course cloth, *Jekker* meaning jacket. Secondly, that it takes its name from p-coat, short for 'pilot's coat' (in days gone by, navigators were called pilots.) With its sturdy construction and anchor buttons the genuine US Navy M21 pea coat looks good, and more importantly its closely woven texture keeps you extremely warm. Sterlingwear of Boston makes pea coats for the US Navy, which are also available to civilians. Pea coats are a serious winter addition to any Ivy wardrobe.

The original duffle coat made by Gloverall was an oversized coat worn by British sailors over their uniforms. In 1951 Gloverall sold their surplus from the Second World War and the Korean War. These surplus duffle coats quickly spread to most countries that had cold winters. They soon became the top coat of choice for British students and ironically, political radicals. In France, Parisian Left Bank existentialists wore the duffle coat as a symbol of anti-bourgeois sentiment. In America it was the opposite; duffle coats were a strictly collegiate affair, and no Ivy League student would leave home without one, often continuing to wear the coat long after leaving college. Many companies now make duffle coats but the original model made by Gloverall is the benchmark. The pea coat and the duffle coat are the ultimate signifiers of the Ivy look in cold weather. *Above:* Jack Nicholson and Art Garfunkel in the 1971 movie *Carnal Knowledge.*

CONTINENTAL DRIFT
From Saint-Germain-des-Pres to the Via Veneto, the Ivy influence prevails

In the *Poste Parisien* recording studios on the night of December 4, 1957, Miles Davis stood in a darkened room in front of a screen onto which film director Louis Malle projected scenes from his debut movie. Davis and solid expatriate drummer Kenny Clarke, plus three Frenchmen – tenor saxophonist Barney Wilen, pianist Rene Urtregar and bassist Pierre Michelot improvised the score as the images played out on the screen. They nailed it in a single session. The black and white movie was a thriller starring Jeanne Moreau and Lino Ventura called *Ascenseur pour L'Echafaud* (Lift to the Scaffold). For Miles Davis and Louis Malle it was a transatlantic meeting of minds, which resulted in the most hauntingly beautiful soundtrack ever produced for any of the French New Wave films. This was the Ivy look set to music, so cool it was sub zero.

Like poachers turned gamekeepers, Francois Truffaut, Jean-Luc Godard, Claude Chabrol, Jacques Rivette and most of the great directors who inhabited the world of French post-war cinema had originally been film critics working on a French journal called *Cahiers du Cinema*. They were obsessed with the individuality of such Hollywood film directors as Orson Welles, Howard Hawks, Alfred Hitchcock and Nicholas Ray.

With the use of hand held camera shots, sudden jump cuts, natural light and outside locations, these celluloid hipsters shattered the rules of conventional movie making. The soundtracks were modern jazz influenced and directors as well as actors were copping the Ivy look. The mannerisms and attitudes of the leading trio of French actors Jean Paul Belmondo, Jean Louis Trintignant and Alain Delon were much copied by knowing Faces from London to Tokyo. It was a moveable feast of corduroy jackets, loafers and trench coats, indeed, in many pockets a navy blue beret nestled alongside a pack of Gitanes.

Opposite: Soul meeting. Director Federico Fellini and his alter ego, actor Marcello Mastroianni, defined the Italian art of living well.

'I like jazz, foreign films, Ivy League clothes, gin and tonic and pretty girls – the same sort of things Playboy readers like'

Hugh Hefner, describing the height of hip in 1957

The distinctive high-pitched buzz of Vespa scooters provided a different kind of soundtrack to the *pavoneggiarsi* (peacock male), who frequented the cafes and bars along Rome's Via Veneto. Italy was always a country where it was not only a privilege but also a responsibility to dress well. This was a given, whatever your position in society. The always elegant Marcello Mastroianni epitomised the Italian style of dress, which to a degree was influenced by the Ivy look, albeit with a smooth Italian accent. This is no surprise as the Italians had most certainly taken note of the clothes worn by the off-duty American GIs stationed there during and after the war.

Modern jazz was also a contributing factor in spreading the Ivy look throughout Italy. Cool school trumpeter Chet Baker and his various quartets had performed in Italy since the early 1950s. Their unmistakable West Coast sound perfectly reflected the pared-down minimal look of the Ivy League clothes Mister Chet wore.

This whole period in Italy's recent past was brilliantly captured by Federico Fellini whose cinematic vision of Rome's high life in his 1960 movie *La Dolce Vita* put the seal of approval on all things Italian. Like the ripples of some great sartorial stone dropped into water, this cross-cultural fertilisation between New York, Paris and Rome eventually reached London, where it was not unusual for some button-down, Ivy wearing Modernists to take an interest in French and Italian newspapers and magazines, to drink espresso coffee and ride Vespa scooters. The American Marshall McLuhan's concept of a Global Village was on schedule.

Opposite: Riding on a new wave. The Italian poster for *à Bout De Souffle* (Breathless), director Jean-Luc Godard's 1959 debut movie starring Jean-Paul Belmondo and American actress Jean Seberg. Belmondo and Seberg's clothes, manners and very cool attitude were a big influence on London's Modernist community.

The French New Wave movie poster for *Ascenseur pour L'Echafaud* (art by Willy Mucha, design by Jacques Fourastie) and *à Bout De Souffle* are telling examples of the response European designers, photographers and illustrators had to American influenced films.

MARCELLO MASTROIANNI · ANITA EKBERG
ANOUK AIMEE · YVONNE FURNEAUX · ALAIN CUNY
ANNIBALE NINCHI · WALTER SANTESSO · MAGALI NOEL
LEX BARKER · JACQUES SERNAS E CON NADIA GRAY

FEDERICO FELLINI
LA DOLCE VITA

TOTALSCOPE MARCHIO DEPOSITATO DALL A.F.C.

UNA CO-PRODUZIONE
RIAMA FILM, ROMA · PATHE CONSORTIUM CINEMA, PARIGI
REALIZZATA DA
GIUSEPPE AMATO

DISTRIBUZIONE

Opposite: The 1960s poster for *La Dolce Vita* brings to life the louche, decadent twilight world of Rome's Via Veneto, inhabited by paparazzi photographers and Roman high life.

Above: The only way to travel. Vespa advertising from the late 1950s.

Francois Truffaut's classic 1960 movie *Tirez Sur Le Pianiste* (Shoot the Piano Player).
With a snap of the fingers, the hip poster art by Jouineau Bourduge transports you to the
ivy cool of 1960s Paris.

Movie director Jean-Pierre Melville's hard hitting 1962 thriller *Le Doulos*, starring Jean-Paul Belmondo, had it all. A cool jazz score, American film noir lighting and trench coats.

Above: For a brief period Miles Davis got into expensive Italian tailoring which probably accounts for him being voted 'Best Dressed Man' in 1961 by *GQ*, the American men's magazine.

Opposite: Chet Baker was briefly imprisoned in Lucca, Italy for drug offences in 1961. Doing time obviously did not cramp his Ivy style as Mister Chet decorates a Christmas tree wearing a flat cap, duffle coat, Levi's and brogues.

HAT CHECK
Hats guaranteed to give you a head start

Hats matter to the Ivy look. Social history would have it that the hat a man wears serves to identify his place or function in society. Ironically, John F. Kennedy who apart from being President of the USA, was by general consensus also Commander-in-Chief of the Ivy League, was rarely seen to wear a hat. Hatless Jack unwittingly caused a certain amount of confusion among some fully paid up Democratic hat wearing Ivy voters. However, to get a real fix on serious hat wearers you have to look to those luminaries of modern jazz, the glue that fuses the connection between music and the Ivy look.

During a 1959 sabbatical from the relentless pressure of recording sessions and club dates, Sonny Rollins was seen practising in the small hours of the morning on the Williamsburg Bridge in New York. On his distinctive shaven head was the hat that has become synonymous with modern jazz – a standard-issue beret. The list of cats in hats is endless, from Gerry Mulligan's back-buckled Ivy League sports cap to Mister chapeau himself, Thelonius Monk. Most nights at the Five Spot, Village Vanguard or any of Manhattan's countless clubs, Monk could be seen wearing a formidable array of hats. Taking care of business in straw coolies, chequered caps and snap-brims, this genius of modern music appeared to have a hat for every tune.

Madison Avenue's tribes of ad men, their narrow brim trilbies firmly in place, and Tinseletown's anti-heroes and bad boys with lids at accepted angles of jauntiness, all these diverse, unlikely fashion plates influenced a generation of hip Ivy Leaguers in the ways of headwear. If you only own one hat it has to be the Brooks Brothers rain hat. Although this hat of tan cotton poplin with its navy and red band does its job with understated style just as well when the sun shines. It is for sure a stone cold Ivy classic.

Jack Lemmon, real name John Uhler Lemmon III, was educated at Harvard which makes him a bona fide Ivy Leaguer. Here Jack wears an excellent corduroy Ivy cap with back-buckle. Perfect. His good friend, film director Billy Wilder sports a more European style tweed driving cap.

ELECTRA $15.95   COMET $11.95

KNOX creates : bronzley

Another fashion-first from Knox. Shades of Bronzley...rich, different, distinguished...will lead the color parade in men's hats this Fall. Bronzley has the antiqued look of finest old bronze...a perfect complement to all the smartest clothing in your Fall wardrobe. This flattering new shade now available in the newest shapes and styles. Knox hats are priced from as little as $11.95 to $50.

KNOX, THE LEADER IN MEN'S HAT FASHIONS SINCE 1838, AT THE BEST STORES IN THE U. S. AND CANADA. A DIVISION OF HAT CORPORATION OF AMERICA

BOXER $11.95

Knox, 1960.

smart tack for a fair heading

KNOX
SUN WEAVES

Knox creates Sun Weaves...straw cool, straw light, straw comfortable. Young salt or landlubber...on deck or on business, there's a Knox Sun Weave for you. Casual or conservative, they're all cool, comfortable — and correct. Knox straws $5.95 to $20.00. ...**man to man it's KNOX SUN WEAVES**

KNOX, THE LEADER IN MEN'S HAT FASHIONS SINCE 1838. AT THE FINEST STORES IN THE UNITED STATES AND CANADA. A DIVISION OF HAT CORPORATION OF AMERICA. PRICES SLIGHTLY HIGHER WEST OF THE ROCKIES.

Knox, 1962.

Gerry Mulligan and his cotton Ivy League sports cap.

Sonny Rollins wearing the hat synonymous with modern jazz – a standard-issue beret.

Above: For the cover of his 1957 Riverside album, *Monk's Music*, Thelonius Monk rides his kiddie car wearing a checked madras cap and a deeply hip pair of sunglasses. Cover photograph by Paul Weller, designed by Paul Bacon.

Opposite: Mister chapeau. The genius of modern music Thelonious Monk plays piano as only he can, wearing a straw coolie.

175 **HAT CHECK**

If you own just one hat it has to be the Brooks Brothers rain hat. Although this hat of tan cotton poplin with its navy and red band does its job with understated style, it also performs just as well when the sun shines. (Used to be also available in navy and white).

Brooks Brothers tartan Ivy cap. Classic plaid cap made from 100% woven wool fabric. An essential addition to any serious hat collection.

New "Shades of Sand"...
new shades of difference in Straw by Dobbs

Inspired by exotic sun cities of the world. Finely hand-crafted, versatile *Dobbs Milan* (lower right) adds elegance to globe trotting. From $11.95. Count on the *Dobbs Panaire* (left), a classic Panama, for that extra touch of distinction. From $10.95. The casual *Dobbs Haiti Palm* (upper right) has the airy flair of a tropical holiday. $5.95. All feature exclusive Dobbs bands. Dobbs straws are available at fine stores throughout the U.S. and Canada.

DOBBS

Dobbs Aruba Palm...the "fun" companion anywhere under the sun. $6.95.

DOBBS, PARK AVENUE AT 45TH ST., NEW YORK, N.Y. *Prices slightly higher west of the Rockies* DOBBS IS A DIVISION OF HAT CORP. OF AMERICA

Dobbs, 1963.

New from Dobbs...the two-tone Gamebird hat with a gift "for her"

It's Fall across the country! Woodsmoke, vivid trees, country drives and Dobbs Gamebird. It's the spirited new Two-Tone* hat with the distinctive look for bright autumn days. Everything about Gamebird warrants attention. Smart contrast coloring that reflects your own sporting individuality...a ribbed brim and band styled for town and country...and a unique pheasant ornament. Dobbs remembers your lady fair, too...with an extra matching pin for her. Dobbs Gamebird hat *and* extra pin for her. $15. Dobbs hats are available at finer stores throughout United States and Canada... $10.95 to $100. Dobbs, Park Ave. at 49th St., N.Y.

*Pat. Pending

"For her." A true-to-life-color pheasant lapel pin that matches the ornament on his band. It's an extra at no extra cost with Dobbs Two-Tone Gamebird $15 hat.

For him. Gamebird in Heather Mixture. Telescope crown, cashmere-soft finish and exclusive ribbed band and brim. $12.95.

DOBBS

B. Peak

DOBBS IS A DIVISION OF HAT CORPORATION OF AMERICA

Above: Dobbs, 1959.

Opposite: The personification of the Ivy look. Paul Newman wears a white back-buckled Ivy cap as it should be worn.

EAST MEETS WEST
East beats West

London had its Modernists, Paris had 'Les Minets' but it was in Tokyo that the 1960s youth 'Ivyquake' was truly manifested with style and precision. A youth cult called 'Miyuki-zoku' sprung up in the summer of 1964 as a response to a new magazine propagating Ivy League style called *Heibon Punch*. As the photographic evidence shows, the kids who adopted the look did so with remarkable verve and attention to detail. Members of the cult would meet up on Miyuki Street bedecked in classic American collegiate gear – button-down oxford cloth shirts, madras plaid, high-water trousers in khaki and white, penny loafers, wing-tip brogues and three button suit jackets. Everything was worn extremely slim.

As often happens when the style transfers to another culture, subtle, beautiful little changes happen which often make the new version more interesting than the original. Such is the case in general when it comes to the Japanese and their love of the Ivy look. And there are many examples of what a long-lasting love it is. It is the Japanese who own America's remaining authentically natural shoulder Ivy retailer J. Press. Yes, the clothes are made in the USA but it is overwhelmingly sold and worn in Japan. It is the Japanese who published *Take Ivy*, an acclaimed collection of photographs of students on Ivy college campuses in 1965 which now sells for four-figure sums and has been endlessly ripped of by hundreds of fashion designers ever since. It is the Japanese who started the Van Jacket clothing company in 1948, still selling impeccable Ivy styled clothes to this day. Company motto: 'For the young and the young-at-heart'. And in recent years it is the Japanese who published two sensational little paperbacks, now sadly out of print but much coveted, called *Ivy Illustrated*. The language gap makes it difficult for westerners to fully appreciate the books' offerings but the beautifully drawn clothes, with hundreds of clothing combinations across the full range of the Ivy style pantheon, are charming and wonderfully comprehensive and precise. Where many have either neglected or slighted the Ivy League look the Japanese enthusiasts have elevated it to new levels of obsession and fetishism and we can only thank and applaud them for it.

The Miyuki-zoku, Tokyo, 1964.

Above: It's All Right! — Wynton Kelly Trio, Verve Records, 1964. Illustration by Russ Gale, cover design by Michael J. Malatak. Roy Lichtenstein gave us his highly inflluential *Whaam!* in 1963. This album, a very hip crossover soul-jazz piece, was released the following year. The influence of the pop art movement was being keenly felt, the ripples of which could still be seen many years later in the type of illustration featured in the *Ivy Illustrated* books.

Opposite: Kazuo Hozumi's excellent book *Ivy Illustrated*, sadly now out of print.

IVY
ILLUSTRATED
絵本アイビーボーイ図鑑

穂積和夫

毎シーズン"着るものがない!"と、お悩みの貴男(あなた)へ
おしゃれの基本はここにあります。

愛育社

IVY CULTURE
AND THE CREATIVE IMPULSE
Music, architecture, art and design

'To me, Beauty is the wonder of wonders... It is only shallow people who do not judge by appearances.' Oscar Wilde's quote chimes with those of us in the Ivy League clothing community. So let's judge. In 1960 John Coltrane and photographer William Claxton paid a visit to the newly constructed Guggenheim Museum. While there Claxton took a series of pictures of Coltrane, just two of which survive. In the first Coltrane is shot face on with the interior structure of the building revealed behind. Claxton has captured Coltrane at his absolute physical and creative peak; handsome and composed, he is soon to produce some of the most profound music of the twentieth century. Did Coltrane himself have any sense of the relationship between his own experiments in structure and form and those so clearly on display in Frank Lloyd Wright's wonderful building? Such a connection is impossible to resist. At the centre of this perfect synthesis of elements is the precision of Coltrane's garb – standard-issue Ivy League given a subversive Modernist inflection by keeping the top button of his jacket buttoned

Opposite: The cover of a 5-CD boxed set from Prestige called *Interplay*, highlighting Coltrane's side-man sessions of the 1950s. This is the seminal picture of Coltrane at the Guggenheim Museum in 1960 in front of a Robert Motherwell painting.

up, an act which instantly distanced his wardrobe choices from the stuffy confines of 'proper' dress. In the other picture from John and Bill's big day out Coltrane is again strikingly juxtaposed with advanced American modernism, this time being framed in front of the bold black abstract slashes of a Robert Motherwell painting.

This was indeed a time when the relationship between faith in the modern and the Ivy wardrobe was distinct and omnipresent. As New York became the centre of the modern art world in the 1950s so the Ivy look became visual shorthand for membership of the various creative factions of the day. A pair of penny loafers quickly shook off strict WASP collegiate affiliation by being adopted by any self-respecting horn-rimmed architect or angst-ridden abstract expressionist. Robert Motherwell regularly painted in just a plain t-shirt, turned-up Levi's, and paint-spattered Weejuns or long wing-tip brogues. Jackson Pollock often slipped into penny loafers to mix up his quintessentially American work wear outfits. Interesting to note too the ironic contrast between the intense spirituality of the work of Mark Rothko and his predilection for wearing a very proper grey herringbone sack jacket. Looking now towards the West Coast, the Modernist impulse there was always expressed in an appropriately upbeat and optimistic way. Perhaps the greatest sunshine designer of all was Charles Eames who has probably produced much of the furniture that those of us at the modernist end of the Ivy spectrum would most like to fill our homes with. Eames always looked like the modern man, unencumbered by tradition and in a hurry to make ordinary people's lives nicer, cleaner and more sophisticated. This sense of purpose was beautifully expressed in his wardrobe choices – the all-American casualness of chinos, loafers, natural shoulder jackets and jaunty bow ties. This clean-cut style was always topped off with that most 1950s and American of hairstyles, the crew cut. The symbiotic relationship between a certain wardrobe and choice of occupation very much lives on. Even today the donning of a pair of Weejuns and a Brooks Brothers button-down operates as a metaphor for creative intent – you are just as likely to be an art director as a college lecturer.

Opposite: Welcome to Dreamsville: 1950s California. One is an imagined vision: the ultimate hipster's apartment suspended high above the lights of the big city a la Neutra or Koenig. The other is very much real: the great Charles Eames' lounge chair and ottoman from 1956. Style, comfort, elegance – form following function. Clothes and design finding strong parallels.

187 IVY CULTURE AND THE CREATIVE IMPULSE

Thelonious Monk Sonny Rollins, Prestige Records 1955. The restrained abstraction
of the 'Contemporary' period here finds beautiful expression in jazz album cover art.
Cover Illustration by Tom Hannan.

Jazz a la Bohemia − Randy Weston Trio. Riverside Records, 1956. Recorded live at the legendary Cafe Bohemia nightclub, Greenwich Village, NYC. The cover photograph by Paul Weller wittily juxtaposes the archetypal beatnik with the dapper Mr Weston but in truth the modern jazz artist and those affiliated to 'beat' culture shared many of the same values and emotional instincts.

REST AND RECREATION
Foreign wheels and a pack of Luckies

When it comes to getting from A to B in some style, East Coast Ivy Leaguers have always been in love with foreign cars. From British MGs and Jaguar XK-120s to Italian Fiats and Ferraris the appeal of European marques will be forever linked to the Ivy look. The most successful set of foreign wheels must surely be the Volkswagen Beetle.

In 1959, Doyle Dane Bernbach, the New York advertising agency, was appointed to handle the Volkswagen account in the USA. They pitched the Beetle's quirkiness as an antidote to the chrome-laden home grown American cars of the period. While Detroit added ever more gimmicks year on year, the Beetle remained the same. This advertising campaign succeeded in convincing the sophisticated eastern establishment it was the car to drive, a kind of protest against built-in obsolescence. It also made the VW Beetle as instantly recognisable as a Coca Cola bottle.

Another classic from the man who gave the world the VW Beetle, the brilliant car designer Ferdinand Porsche, was the beautiful Porsche 356 Speedster. With its charismatic smooth lines it won over battalions of discerning American GIs stationed in Germany, so much so that the returning servicemen shipped many of the Speedsters back to the USA. In the early 1960s, driving down the Massachusetts Turnpike from Boston to Cape Cod in a Porsche 356 Speedster, Ivy cap firmly in place and Baracuta G9 Harrington zipped up against the wind, must have given those lucky owners a real buzz.

We know better now but in the 1950s and 1960s everybody smoked. Tobacco companies sponsored television and radio shows and magazines were full of adverts extolling the virtues of the various brands of cigarettes. The designs that adorned the soft packs and cartons that cigarettes came in were very seductive; they were part of the culture.

With its distinctive mechanical click and simplicity of design the Zippo lighter has achieved cult status, even among those who do not smoke. Based on an Austrian Army lighter and completely wind-proof, George Blaisdell created the original Zippo in 1932. It was an instant success, the classic shape virtually unchanged, indeed, every Zippo sold still comes with the guarantee 'It works or we fix it free'!

An American classic. The legendary Zippo lighter was sold in its millions.

The restrained typography and exotically distinctive illustration on a pack of Camel was very seductive.

The design of the Marlboro pack by Frank Gianninoto in the 1950s was an instant success. With its bold red, black and white graphics Marlboro soon became a market leader.

Gitanes and Gauloises were the preferred smoke of the French New Wave congregation and many London Modernists. A certain M. Ponty is credited for the unique blue and white design of the Gitanes pack.

Opposite: Ivy clothes and a pack of Luckies. Lucky Strike advertisement from the early 1960s. Former fashion illustrator and prolific product designer, Raymond Loewy created the Lucky Strike pack in 1941.

Above: Actor and trophy winning race driver Paul Newman and his 1963 Volkswagen convertible in a promotional brochure for Volkswagen. Newman assiduously avoided the movie star image of flashy, expensive sports cars, although his various convertible Beetles were rumoured to be equipped with Porsche engines!

Opposite: Porsche advertising was always ahead of the curve as this impressive brochure cover for the 1955 Speedster suggests. It is no surprise that American GIs serving in Germany were smitten with the beautiful lines of the Speedster.

Above: German engineering meets Italian styling. The very cool, head turning Karman Ghia Coupe from Volkswagen.

Opposite: The Ivy approved all-American Ford Mustang made famous in the hands of the uber cool Steve McQueen in the 1968 movie *Bullit*.

1966 Mustang

1966 Mustang Hardtop

If you thought we couldn't improve on a winner —try Mustang '66!

The changes are subtle but significant. A new grille for a bright, fresh front-end look. New options like the Stereo-sonic tape system. (It gives you over 70 minutes of music on an easy-loading tape cartridge.) All the wonderful features that made Mustang a success are still standard. After all, why change Mustang in mid-stream?

The '66 Mustang comes with bucket seats, all-vinyl interiors, floor-mounted shift, full carpeting and many other luxuries at no extra cost. It is an exceptionally practical car with its lively 200-cubic-inch Six. It handles like a candidate for the Monte Carlo Rallye and is so handsome it tends to make anything near its price look tired. This is the basic Mustang.

But if you want more action, greater luxury, Mustang offers you an exceptional range of options. You can design your own sports-Mustang with GT options like front disc brakes; 289-cubic-

inch Cobra V-8 with four-barrel carburetor and solid lifters; four-speed, fully-synchronized manual transmission or 3-speed Cruise-O-Matic—and more. Luxury-lovers can have air-conditioning, power brakes and steering, vinyl-covered top, or a specially elegant interior décor package....just to name a few.

If you haven't driven a Mustang yet ...do it soon. It's bound to improve your outlook on driving.

MUSTANG!
MUSTANG!
MUSTANG!

STEVE McQUEEN
The best-dressed bad boy in Hollywood

Wearing a navy blue cashmere turtleneck sweater, brown tweed Ivy jacket and still to this day, the most sought after pair of brown suede, crepe soled boots; Steve McQueen set the standard for Ivy cool as the anti-hero cop in the movie *Bullitt.* He was the hippest police lieutenant ever to hit the streets of San Francisco. Not only did McQueen look pin sharp in *Bullitt,* he also got to drive a very fast, drab green 1967 390 GT fastback Mustang. It was the Ivy look on speed.

Movies have always had a habit of elevating every day objects and clothes to cult status. On a big screen, even the smallest details become as glamorous and cool as the stars that wear them. In *The Thomas Crown Affair,* Steve McQueen's favourite picture – originally a story written by Boston attorney Alan Trustman, McQueen was transformed brilliantly into character, perfectly groomed down to the last detail, wearing a series of softly tailored, immaculate Ivy style formal suits by Beverley Hills tailor, Ron Postal. Off set McQueen was certainly no slouch in the sartorial department. His wardrobe was brim full of the finest Ivy classics. From short-sleeve seersucker button-down shirts and needle cord, cross pocket, fourteen-inch bottom trousers to that iconic shawl-collared cardigan and 501 Levi's, battered and faded to perfection from riding his beloved motorcycle.

During the early 1960s photographer and friend of Steve McQueen, William Claxton, took some memorable shots of Mr S and guess what? In nearly every one he was wearing those trademark brown suede boots that he wore in *Bullitt.* A fortune is probably waiting to be made if any boot maker out there can exactly replicate those boots. In an interview McQueen once said 'I am a limited actor. My range isn't that great and I don't have that much scope. I'm pretty much myself most of the time in my movies.' He may not have had the range of Laurence Olivier but he looked better in a Baracuta G9 Harrington jacket and Persol sunglasses at the wheel of his beautiful 1966 Ferrari 275 GTS than the entire coterie of Hollywood's leading actors.

Opposite: Free wheeling. Steve McQueen set the standard for Ivy cool on and off the movie set.

ENGLAND

Above: Most famously worn by Steve McQueen, the incomparable G9 Baracuta waist length jacket with its trademark Fraser clan tartan lining. Connoisseurs of the Ivy look know it as the Harrington. In 1937 John Miller and Brothers started making the original G9 Baracuta at Chorlton Street warehouse in Manchester, England. From Ivy Leaguers to Mods, the G9 has justifiably achieved cult status and is without doubt a contemporary classic.

Opposite: An advance poster for the 1968 movie *Bullitt*.

SHOP AROUND
Where to find the good stuff: retailers, makers and websites

RETAILERS

American Classics, 20 Endell Street, London, WC2.
www.americanclassicslondon.com
Part of the landscape for Americana enthusiasts since 1981 American Classics does what it says on the tin. Once a key destination to source great vintage gear, the emphasis nowadays is on authentic new denim products, in particular the great Made in USA 'Levi Vintage' range. You'll also find strong brands like Red Wing, Barracuta, Dockers and Sugar Cane.

The Andover Shop, 22 Holyoke Street, Cambridge, Massachusetts and 2 branches.
www.theandovershop.com
If it doesn't already it surely ought to have a plaque on it announcing that it was on this spot in 1954 that Charlie Davidson introduced Miles to Ivy style '…a look that redefined cool and shook those who thought they were in the know' according to Miles' biographer John Szwed.

Brooks Brothers, 346 Madison Avenue, New York City and many other outlets.
www.brooksbrothers.com
They still make the shirt, the original soft collar oxford cloth Made in USA button-down, and sell the shoes, the unlined Horween shell cordovan penny loafer made for them by Alden. An iconic retailer for all fans of Ivy League style.

John Rushton Shoes, 93 Wimpole Street, London, W1.
www.johnrushtonshoes.com
The charismatic Mr Rushton is a man of some style and distinction. The carefully selected range concentrates primarily on fine English shoemaking brands but there are also interesting American and French offerings. The shop also provides probably the best shoe repairing service in London.

J. Press, 380 Madison Avenue, New York City and other outlets.
www.jpressonline.com
The other original Ivy retailer, Press make much of the authentic American provenance of most of their stock, for which they must be applauded. They once used to sell a wonderful shirt with a rather controversial flap on the breast pocket and one day, who knows, they may do so once again?

L.L. Bean, Main Street, Freeport, Maine.
www.llbean.com

A celebrated feature of WASP New England outdoor culture, the famous Bean Boot is, thankfully, still handcrafted in Maine. Some decent bits and pieces elsewhere too. Their famous catalogues and a comprehensive website back up a huge mail order operation.

Murray's Toggery Shop, 62 Main Street, Nantucket Island, MA.
www.nantucketreds.com
If you are in New England and find yourself on Cape Cod, catch the boat to Nantucket Island, it's worth the visit for this is the home of the famous Nantucket Reds and much more.

O'Connells, 3240 Main Street, Buffalo, New York state.
www.oconnellsclothing.com
Gloriously traditional, O'Connells carries a great range of the very best quality items from the very best manufacturers. They also have many hard-to-find items including authentic bleeding madras shirts. Great customer service from their mail order department.

Paul Stuart, Madison Avenue at 45th street, New York City.
www.paulstuart.com

Geographically, historically and psychologically connected with the greats of Brooks and Press this member of the triptych offers luxury traditional style with more of a European sensibility in the mix. They famously eschew 3 button sack and have long pioneered a 2 button opening with a natural shoulder. We just about forgive them.

Ralph Lauren, 1 New Bond Street, London W1 and numerous branches.
www.ralphlauren.co.uk
Now a huge global brand Ralph Lauren must be applauded for keeping elements of the Ivy League aesthetic alive during the bleak years of the 1970s. That vision may now be rather diluted but there are always good things to be found in his shops and the commitment to proper shoulder line and traditional materials remains.

Uniqlo *www.uniqlo.co.uk*
Japan's leading clothing retailer now has 14 shops in the UK and many more worldwide. To the diligent Ivy orientated shopper they frequently offer authentically-styled natural shoulder jackets and good quality affordable knitwear and sweatshirts. Someone at Uniqlo knows what's what. Always a shop worth keeping an eye on.

MAKERS

Alden, 344 Madison Avenue at 44th street, New York City.
www.aldenshoe.com
Many of the great old firms have gone, or impoverished the quality of their goods through outsourcing. Praise be that Alden, America's greatest shoemaker, continues to make wonderful Ivy League classics, including the majestic cordovan leather range, in their New England headquarters.

Bill's Khakis, Reading, Pennsylvania.
www.billskhakis.com
Khakis the way they used to be made. The whole point about Bill's Khakis is that they are a proper Made in USA trouser made to last and get better as they age.

J. Keydge, 1-3 Rue de l'Arcade, 75008 Paris.
www.jkeydge.com
Manufacturers of the excellent 's(l)ack jacket' a kind of deconstructed Ivy League jacket, taking the principle of soft shoulder and lack of lining and body to its logical conclusion. At their best Keydge jackets manage to combine the ease and comfort of your favourite cardigan with the elegance of Kind of Blue-era Miles. Well, almost. They're that rare thing – an update of Ivy style which captures the magic of the original stuff.

Mercer and Sons, Yarmouth, Maine.
http://mercerandsons.com
Mercer is to the button-down shirt what Bill's is to khakis: a back to basics, uncompromisingly good and justifiably expensive Made in USA product that doesn't cut corners. 'Baggier and better' runs their slogan and they successfully produce a shirt of impeccable material selection and perfect collar roll.

WEBSITES

A Continuous Lean
http://acontinuouslean.com
Well designed and well written website that celebrates and seeks to revive a particular sort of American aesthetic. Great taste in clothes and proudly flying the flag for Made in USA products of all descriptions.

Film Noir Buff

www.filmnoirbuff.com

Particularly famed for its lively 'Talk Ivy' forum in which Ivy enthusiasts of all nationalities and affiliations come together to dissect the intricacies of the look. You'll come across real experts here displaying impressive depth of knowledge but the overall tone is welcoming and celebratory.

Garmsville

http://garmsville.blogspot.com

Run by British hipster, man about town and serious Ivy enthusiast Jason Jules, Garmsville celebrates and elevates street fashion and culture with distinctive, intelligent style.

The Ivy League Look

http://theivyleaguelook.blogspot.com

This is a regularly updated and brilliantly researched blog that regularly comes up trumps with little known but wonderful vintage ads from a range of original sources. The natural shoulder period has truly found its perfect archivist.

Ivy Style

www.ivy-style.com

Always lively and well written Ivy Style explores our favourite subject with probing thoughtfulness. Has produced some great features including an illuminating interview with Ivy style guru G. Bruce Boyer.

Mister Mort

http://mistermort.typepad.com

Mort follows the 'Sartorialist' route, snapping interesting-looking folk on the street, but exhibits a refreshingly non-elitist approach, taking particular delight in quirky outfits rooted in traditional Americana.

RIP: Gone but not forgotten

American Gentlemen, Austins, Buffalo Creek Traders shoes, Chipp, Dexter, Eastland, The Ivy Shop, J. Simons, Sero, Troy Shirtmakers Guild, Walk Over, Wilkes.

ACKNOWLEDGEMENTS

A tip of the beret to:

John Simons, June Marsh, Glyn Callingham, Tony Nourmand,
Suzie and Keith Cunningham, The Crew from the Island, Mark Collins,
Mr Isaacs, Jim Kenny, Sean Kenny, Phil Stedman, Max and Coco Katz,
Nicki Davis, Sam the cat, Richard Riddick, David Cutts and Andrew Dunn.

Many thanks to:

Brooks Brothers, J. Press, Blue Note Records, EMI, *Esquire* magazine,
Verve Records, G.H. Bass & Co., Florsheim Shoes, L.L.Bean, Sperry, Jack Purcell,
Converse, Alden Shoes, Gant shirt makers, Pacific Jazz Records,
Contemporary Records, Galey & Lord, McGregor, Van Heusen, RCA Victor,
Atlantic Records, Ralph Lauren, Riverside Records, Lee Jeans, Fantasy Records,
Clarks Shoes, Vespa, Lambretta, Imperial Records,
John Fitzgerald Library, Boston, Catalina, Levi's, Lacoste, John Smedley,
Pendleton shirts, Kazuo Hozumi, Columbia Records, Prestige Records,
Charles Eames, Zippo Lighters, Camel, Marlboro, Gitanes, Lucky Strike,
Volkswagen, Porsche, Ford Motors, Baracuta.

Photographic credits: The Kobal Collection: 8, 15, 38, 74, 82, 155, 198.
Camera Press: 10. Lebrecht Music & Arts: 49. Steve Schapiro: 106, 107.
The DPC: 51, 116, 117, 143. Getty Images: 72, 157.
Robert Knudsen: 133. Everett Collection: 169.
Movie Posters: 17, 101, 159, 160, 161, 162, 164, 165, 200 all courtesy of
The Reel Poster Gallery.
Illustrations by Graham Marsh: 27, 33, 34, 42, 43, 52, 53, 54, 55, 76, 77, 105.
Apologies to anyone we've inadvertently missed out, of which we are sure
there are many. Every effort has been made to trace and credit
photographers where possible.